FACES ON THE EDGE

FACES

TYPE IN THE

DESIGNED BY MICHAEL IAN KAYE

THE DIGITAL EDGE

STEVEN HELLER AND ANNE FINK

VAN NOSTRAND REINHOLD
A Division of International Thomson Publishing Inc.
I(T)P®

New York • Albany • Bonn • Boston • Detroit
London • Madrid • Melbourne • Mexico City • Paris
San Francisco • Singapore • Tokyo • Toronto

Cover and Interior Design: Michael Kaye

Van Nostrand Reinhold Staff
Editor: Jane Degenhardt
Production Editor: Carla Nessler
Manufacturing Manager: Mary McCartney

For more information, contact:

Van Nostrand Reinhold
115 Fifth Avenue
New York, NY 10003

Chapman & Hall GmbH
Pappelallee 3
69469 Weinheim
Germany

Chapman & Hall
2-6 Boundary Row
London
SE1 8HN
United Kingdom

International Thomson Publishing Asia
221 Henderson Road #05-10
Henderson Building
Singapore 0315

Thomas Nelson Australia
102 Dodds Street
South Melbourne, 3205
Victoria, Australia

International Thomson Publishing Japan
Hirakawacho Kyowa Building, 3F
2-2-1 Hirakawacho
Chiyoda-ku, 102 Tokyo
Japan

Nelson Canada
1120 Birchmount Road
Scarborough, Ontario
Canada M1K 5G4

International Thomson Editores
Seneca 53
Col. Polanco
11560 Mexico D.F. Mexico

Library of Congress Cataloging-in-Publication Data

Heller, Steven
   Faces on the edge : type in the digital age / Steven Heller and Anne Fink : designed by Michael Ian Kaye.
     p.   cm.
   Included indexes.
   ISBN 0-442-02254-9
   1. Computer fonts. I. Fink, Anne. II. Title.
Z250.7.H45 1997
686.2'24—dc21

96-37962
CIP

http://www.vnr.com
product discounts • free email newsletters
software demos • online resources

email: info@vnr.com

A service of I(T)P®

TO W.A. DWIGGINS, RENAISSANCE MAN: HE MIGHT HAVE HATED THIS BOOK, BUT ADMIRED ITS SPIRIT.

Many people cooperated and assisted to make this book happen. But there would be no book if not for our editor at Van Nostrand Reinhold, Jane Degenhardt—our thanks for her enthusiasm and patience. Michael Ian Kaye, who designed this book, was our most valuable asset. He transformed a collection of disparate materials into a total work with a unique character—our appreciation for a superb job.

We are also grateful to Jane DiBucci, who produced the book for us: Her skill, know-how, and good instincts are immeasurable. Without her there would be no book. Thanks to Rodrigo Corral, who helped organize and oversee the materials on our end. On the Van Nostrand side: Thanks to Carla Nessler for production expertise.

We also take pleasure in acknowledging the many people at the various foundries who generously provided fonts and information and without whom this book would not be possible: first, Rudy VanderLans and Zusana Licko, the real pioneers of digital typefounding and the biological parents of all these faces on the edge. Gratitude goes to Chester at Thirstype, Colin Davis and Carlos Segura at T-26, Betsy Kopshina at Garage Fonts, Joshua Berger at Plazm Media, Tobias Frere-Jones, Jonathan Hoefler at the Hoefler Foundry, Michael Worthington at Cookin' Fonts, Brian Horner at the American Type Corp., Rich Roat at House Industries, Brian Kelly and Nancy Mazzei at Smokebomb, Joshua Distler at Shift, Erik van Bleckland at LettError, Elliot Earls at The Apollo Program, Charles Wilkin at ProtoType, Bob Auldufish at fontBoy, Gary Hustwit and Chank Diesel at Exploding Font Company, Steve Miller, Jurgen Siebert, Stuart Jenson, and T.T. Mai-Linh at FontShop International, Jeffery Keedy, Paul Sync, Sam Pratt, P. Scott Makella, and Margaret Richardson at *U&lc*.

Finally, thanks to all the designers whose work has given shape to this era of digital typesetting.

—Steven Heller and Anne Fink

ACKNOWLEDGMENTS

CONTENTS

FACES ON THE EDGE

TRAWLING THROUGH THE CRITIQUES OF TYPOGRAPHY PUBLISHED IN PRO-FESSIONAL JOURNALS FROM THE EARLY TWENTIETH CENTURY, ONE FINDS A HIGH DEGREE OF CONTEMPT TOWARD THE NEW AND NOVEL. IF CURRENT TYPEFACES SEEM HARSHLY SCRUTI-NIZED BY KEEPERS OF TODAY'S TYPO-GRAPHIC CANON, JUST READ SOME OF THE SCREEDS FROM THE LITANY OF TEMPESTUOUS CONDEMNATIONS PUBLISHED HALF A CENTURY AGO. MORE CENSORIOUS THAN TODAY'S COMMENTARIES, THE VINTAGE REPROACHES ASSAIL WHAT WERE THEN CON-SIDERED MONSTROSITIES OF TYPOGRAPHY (A FEW OF WHICH ARE DEEMED CLASSIC TODAY). IN THE EARLY 1930S FREDERIC EHRLICH, A

DESIGN TEACHER AND UNFORGIVING OPPO-
NENT OF TYPOGRAPHIC INTEMPERANCE,
DENOUNCED THE DECORATIVE EXCESSES IN
THE TYPE OF HIS DAY AS "DYNAMIC INDIGES-
TION...UNREASONED AND RIOTOUS COMPOSI-
TION." AROUND THE SAME TIME, DOUGLAS C.
McMURTRIE, A WELL-KNOWN SCHOLAR AND
OCCASIONAL TYPE DESIGNER HIMSELF,
EXHORTED AGAINST TYPOGRAPHIC MOD-
ERNISM: "[U]NFORTUNATELY [IT] LENDS
ITSELF READILY TO THE DERIVATION OF UNIN-
TELLIGENT FORMULAS." AND IN 1940 DESIGNER
AND PUNDIT T. M. CLELAND MOANED: "THE
EMBARRASSING INEPTITUDE OF THE CURRENT
EFFORTS TOWARD A NEW TYPOGRAPHY ARE
EVEN MORE DISTRESSING THAN SIMILAR CON-
TORTIONS IN OTHER FIELDS. TYPOGRAPHY IS A

servant of thought and language. When there are new ways of thinking . . . and a new language it will be time enough for a new typography. I suggest that those who cannot abide the conventions of typography are mostly those who have never tried them."

These and their fellow critics pledged allegiance to the rightness of form—truth, beauty, and, above all, legibility—a catechism impervious to stylistic heresy. Yet between the carefully composed lines and generous margins in which these statements were presented was a stubborn rejection of all new ideas. The mere suggestion that as times had changed, type should change as well was worse than unacceptable—it was a sin. Equating type with language, the standard bearers proclaimed type as sacrosanct.

During the years between the World Wars graphic design was in flux. In the typographic realm, adherence to traditional typefaces provided continuity with the past and was a bulwark against radical practice. Nevertheless, in Europe the futurists, dadaists, and constructivists were zealously overturning timeworn conventions. The insurgents believed that classical tenets of balance and harmony resulted in moribund design. Overhaul of outmoded systems was desperately needed. They developed a new canon—the New Typography—that challenged the antiquated rules and standards. Serifs were prohibited and central axis composition was banned. Yet the old guard continued to resist, holding firm to the tenets that were

bequeathed them by the early typemasters Jenson, Bodoni, and Didot. These tenets, they argued, could never be sacrificed to the whims of fashion. So the battle lines were drawn between generations, movements, individuals, and schools. The vitriolic and emotional debates ran on and on—just like today.

There is nothing like type to ignite heated arguments among graphic designers. If they cannot be passionate about type—the *lingua franca* of the profession—then what? Dingbats? Diecuts? QuarkXPress? Black matte? If a designer doesn't feel devoutly for type, then he or she is not a devout designer. Assuming religious proportions, type has fundamentalist believers, catholic reformers, and heretical zealots. Type itself may often be neutral, but few are neutral about type.

Type is the designer's tool for communicating ideas. It turns characters into words and words into messages. It is the expression of thought, mood, and emotion. Typefaces are charged with symbolic powers—some even represent behavorial extremes (German Fraktur, for example, is forever associated with the evil of Nazi Germany). To a nondesigner it may seem trivial; how can a mere typeface be so volatile? But in addition to type's functional and stylistic manifestations, it is a repository of history, ideology, and dogma.

Nevertheless, such heightened sensitivity to typographic issues inevitably fosters arcane debates. Legibility, for example, is not usually discussed as just a functional matter but rather as an article of faith. The perfect typeface, say the keepers of tradition, is one that can be easily read (in the traditional way), while a typeface that offers even the slightest roadblock to immediate comprehension is not merely imperfect, it is corrupt. Perhaps the rightness of form is better left to sages because in the flush of passion designers' arguments often devolve into how many typefaces will fit on the head of a pin and can still be flawlessly read.

It is axiomatic that each new era of type design and typesetting is met with varying degrees of suspicion and reticence by those who are tied to the old methods. When phototype was introduced in the early 1950s, Aaron Burns, the patriarch of modern type marketing, took great pains to convince hot metal diehards of the viability of this new method. Although it was easy to prove beyond a shadow of a doubt that phototype was cheaper, faster, and cleaner than hot metal composition, he further had to convince users that the aesthetic quality was far superior. This proved to be entirely subjective. So Burns subtly shifted the focus of his argument. Although the new technology could duplicate hot metal typefaces, it could go much further toward changing—or modernizing—the standards of typography. Among other assets, phototypesetting allowed for closer spacing (touching of letters) and overlapping. Techniques that were difficult and discouraged in hot metal were easy and encouraged through the new technology. It took Burns a long time to convince type directors at advertising agencies and publishing houses that times had changed and so had type design. In the end the new technology prevailed and styles shifted accordingly. The masters of phototypography (notably Herb Lubalin) proved that there were aesthetic virtues to the squeezed, smashed, overlapping, and optically distorted type design of the day.

Phototype was the typographic standard for almost thirty years until the advent of the personal computer in the 1980s, when it gave way to a new typography. Digital technology had a revolutionary effect that once again challenged accepted standards. This time there was an even more fundamental difference in type design and practice. Phototype allowed for more or less faithful reproduction of classical and novel typefaces. When the Macintosh premiered (even before high-resolution output was economically feasible) default type was limited to certain highly pixelated faces. Many type veterans rejected this aberration, while others sought ways of adapting old notions to the new medium. Matthew Carter at Bitstream, a pioneer digital type foundry, designed faces for the computer that were firmly rooted in tradition while expanding its boundaries. Sumner Stone at Adobe Systems, which pioneered graphic design software, such as Illustrator and PhotoShop, established a type design department that developed new and adapted classical forms. At first, the steps were cautiously incremental. But just as movable type, which was developed in the fifteenth century, forever changed the character of letterforms, so digital typefounding changed the basic aesthetics of late twentieth-century type design.

It took prescience to realize that digital type founding would become the state of the art. It took courage to design type that defied convention—that both took advantage of and reveled in the limitations of the Macintosh. This was the terrain that Rudy VanderLans and Zuzana Licko staked out when in 1984 they published, edited, and designed *Emigre,* one of the first tabloid magazines produced on the Macintosh. This arts and culture magazine (which in 1988, with issue #9, was transformed into the clarion of contemporary avant-garde graphic design) required a distinctive look to separate it from other hip tabloids known as *culturetabs;* Macintosh-generated typography was VanderLans and Licko's métier. The typefaces were rough and primitive-looking, but decidedly of the moment and distinctly individual. Macintosh was the tool of the future and coarse resolution typefaces such as *Emigre's* Oakland Six, Eight, Ten, and Fifteen, Universal Nineteen and Eight, and Emigre Fifteen, Nineteen, and Eight (all designed in 1985, before PostScript was introduced), quickly became the typographic symbols of the new age. In 1985, when Emigre Graphics (later called Emigre Fonts) began selling their "fonts," the public and digital era in typography was officially launched.

The advent of the computer language PostScript in 1986, and the introduction of high-resolution image-setters, such as the Linotronic, made typesetting more viable in the digital realm. It also introduced typographic options that were previously inconceivable. During the eras of hot metal and phototype graphic designers usurped the role of type designer now and then, but type design remained a craft-oriented, skill-based field impervious to dilettantes. The new technology changed all that. As novice (but trained) type designers entered the field, so did naïfs and what might be termed guerrilla designers, those who viewed digital type like hand-lettering or graffiti—something ephemeral and not governed by typographic standards. With the rapid development of advanced typesetting and type design software, customized typefaces were not only possible but countless permutations were inevitable. As more graphic designers began designing their own alphabets, digital foundries, such as Font Bureau and FontShop International courted them as prospective contributors. The *fontographers,* as the new breed of type designers is called, were prodigious; during the early nineties new digital cuts were pumped out at a fevered pitch. Faithful digitizations as well as revivals of classic and vintage faces and original new designs were flowing into the market. Out of this upheaval came experimental type.

Emigre was (and continues to be) the wellspring of experimentation, testing and pushing the boundaries of type on various fronts: legibility, balance, color, etc. Following *Emigre's* lead, FUSE, the first digital laboratory for type, was an outlet for research into type form and function. Many FUSE types were ostensibly functional, but some of the more adventuresome experiments were only works-in-progress designed to test the tolerance of accepted reading habits. The publication of these experiments inspired others to enter the fray. In the early 1990s, designers contracted by the nascent foundries realized that computer technology (font-making software and Internet communications) made it possible for anybody to design digital type and establish a foundry. Thus new type houses opened along the information highway (or at least issued catalogs distributed by snail mail); T-26, Thirstype, Garage Fonts, and fontBoy are among those that, in Emigre's footsteps, developed libraries of original, often edgy, weird, and eccentric alphabets and dingbats.

Like those ancient stone carvings that served as the basis for the old master's type designs, these eccentric digital faces were inspired by various historical and contemporary sources. In the post modern ethos they were comments on the cultural environment. Barry Deck's Template Gothic, the *sine qua non* of the new typography, was inspired by a crude sign, seen hanging in a Laundromat, that was drawn using a common plastic template found in stationery stores. Tobias Frere-Jones's Interstate was influenced by the Gothic letters on American interstate highway signs; his Garage Gothic was based on letters extrapolated from common garage receipts. Jonathan Hoefler's Gestalt is the typographic parable of Jungian theory. P. Scott Makela's Dead History signaled the end of an era of traditionally produced fonts and personifies the hybrid typefaces that are the result of the computer's capabilities. And Frank Heine's Motion, a squiggly doodle-like alphabet, was done, he once explained, just for the "pure fun" of it.

Theory plays a role in the design of contemporary typefaces, but the play instinct—pure fun, as Heine suggests—accounts for the majority of faces on the edge. Play is what accounts for most of type history's most novel faces. Back in the sixties, Victor Moscoso, the innovative psychedelic poster artist and letterer, realized that nostalgic alphabets could easily be transformed into contemporary ones by playing with weight, balance, and color combinations. While serious in his work, the process was not based on in-depth perceptual analysis but rather on what felt right and looked good within a certain visual framework. Similarly, today's fontographers intuitively test the Macintosh's programmatic capabilities until finding the most pleasing (or irritating) forms. The computer tempts designers to explore letter-making that rarely surfaced with previous technologies. The perpetually degrading font, or the font that throws out visual noise, or the font that never repeats the same letter twice—these are a few new ways of designing (and playing with) alphabets and typography.

Artists have long flirted with letterforms, using them in paintings and collages. Now, with the democratization (an overused but accurate term) and widespread availability of fonts (a once arcane but now common term) as well as the increased accessibility of the computer as a powerful graphics tool, type has become an artistic medium in its own right. During the late twentieth century, art pushed about as many boundaries as it could. The digital realm is, therefore, new terrain for the artist, and type is a significant part of that landscape. A new breed of artist, weaned on pop culture and nourished by mass media, has embraced type design as a virgin territory. Experimental typefaces are the nexus where art and commerce meet, where a commercial tool becomes a means for pure expression. Many of the most eccentric (dare we say abstract?) typefaces of recent years are visions of individuals creating form ostensibly for themselves. Elliot Earls is one who uses print as a canvas and type like paint to make both word pictures and abstract designs. Of course, type is invariably made for public use, but many of the new typefaces are prescribed for a particular user who subscribes to, or is sympathetic with, the vision of the artist.

Typefaces should no longer be judged by the standards of past generations. Language may not have changed as radically as T. M. Cleland would have wanted for a new typography to be acceptable, but attitudes about the nature of type and typography have. The quirky, often witty names of most contemporary faces reveal both sarcasm and skepticism of the orthodoxy of type. Sure, for many contemporary critics the majority of typefaces surveyed in this book are anathema to the tenets of good design. Many are indeed too weird for any long-term use. But perhaps type has been sacrosanct for too long. Perhaps, neutrality is no longer the virtue. Perhaps in an age of media noise, the louder the statement, the more attention it will get. Probably the majority of these typefaces are stylistic blips, as emblematic of today as Bifur was in the thirties or Busorama was in the sixties. The ubiquity of Emigre's doodle-like typeface Remedy, for example, is for the nineties what Avant Garde was for the seventies and Benguiat was for the eighties. But, just maybe, some of these faces, out of the countless hundreds that are produced and made available through the Web, will endure the test of time. These experiments force both typemakers and type users to address alternative ways of seeing letterforms and to reject or accept them.

Faces on the Edge is not the definitive study of digital typefounding of the nineties. It is, however, a representative survey of what is undeniably a significant era of type design, an era that celebrates idiosyncrasy. This is an interim history of type and of the individuals who command a new medium and have created a design ethos that is of and about its time.

—Steven Heller

FACES ON THE EDGE

ReBIRTHS

TYPE DESIGN IS THE MOST RETRO OF ALL THE DESIGN DISCIPLINES. REVIVALS OF HISTORICAL AND REPRISES OF PASSÉ ALPHABETS COMPRISE A LARGE PERCENTAGE OF THE MAJOR TYPE LIBRARIES. WHENEVER A NEW MEDIUM COMES ALONG THERE IS A MAD DASH TO RECAST, REVISE, AND REINTRODUCE THE MOST POPULAR TYPEFACES AND TO REDISCOVER SOME OF THE LONG-FORGOTTEN ONES TOO. THE ANALOGY TO COMPACT DISKS IS APT: THE SURGE IN DIGITALLY REMIXED ALBUMS CHANGED THE MUSIC INDUSTRY; LIKEWISE, THE TYPE INDUSTRY SAW THE HANDWRITING (OR TYPESETTING) ON THE WALL. DIGITALIZATION MARKED THE END OF PHOTOTYPESETTING. DIGITAL FOUNDRIES STARTED REVIVING AS MANY FACES AS POSSIBLE. BEFORE THE

& CONTEMPORARY FACES HIT THE STREET, TRADITIONAL AS WELL AS NOSTALGIC AND RETRO FACES WERE THERE FIRST.

THE MAJORITY OF REBIRTHS AND REVIVALS IN THIS SECTION ARE NOT CLASSICALLY DERIVED BUT RATHER DRAWN FROM THE HALF DOZEN OR SO STYLISTIC MOVEMENTS AND MANIFESTATIONS TO HAVE HIT TYPE DESIGN SINCE THE LATE NINETEENTH CENTURY. THE EMPHASIS, HOWEVER, IS ON THE BABY BOOM PAST, WITH REPRISES OF TYPES AND LETTER-ING DEFINING THE POPULUX, PSYCHEDELIC, AND DISCO PERIODS. A HYBRIDIZATION OF STYLES ULTIMATELY CONTRIBUTES TO THE ORIGINAL FACES FOUND IN OTHER SECTIONS OF THIS BOOK.

Revivals

A B C D E

F G H I J

K L M N O

P Q R S T

U V W X Y

Z & ? % !

1 2 3 4 5

6 7 8 9 0

RANDUMHOUSE (1995)

ALLEN MERCER

HOUSE INDUSTRIES

Rooted in a late fifties animated cartoon aesthetic, Randumhouse is a whimsical combination of tall and short, upper- and lowercase characters that can be alternated to create numerous combinations.

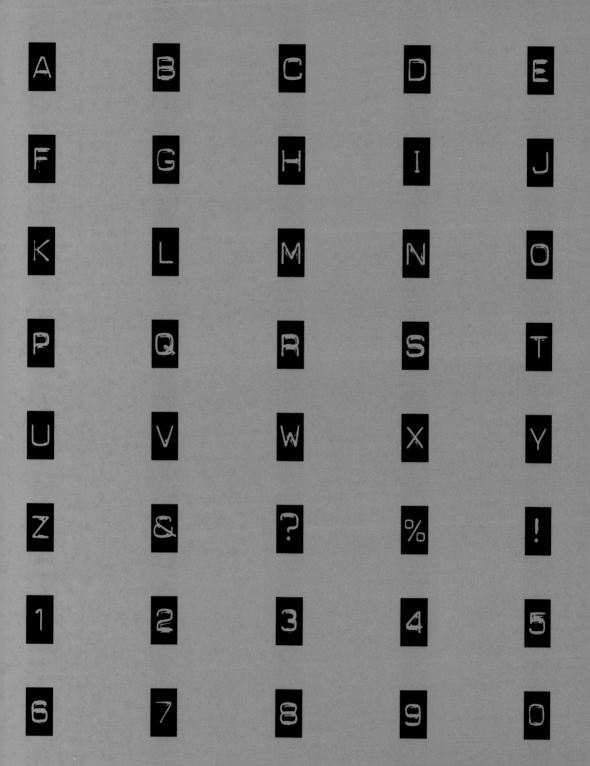

FF DYNAMOE (1992)

JUST VAN ROSSUM

FONTSHOP INTERNATIONAL

The designer had a fascination for vernacular typefaces like Karton, Stamp Gothic, Confidential, and FlightCase. Scanners and outliners made it possible to make digital renderings of the fonts in high detail. Dynamo was taken from a punch label machine.

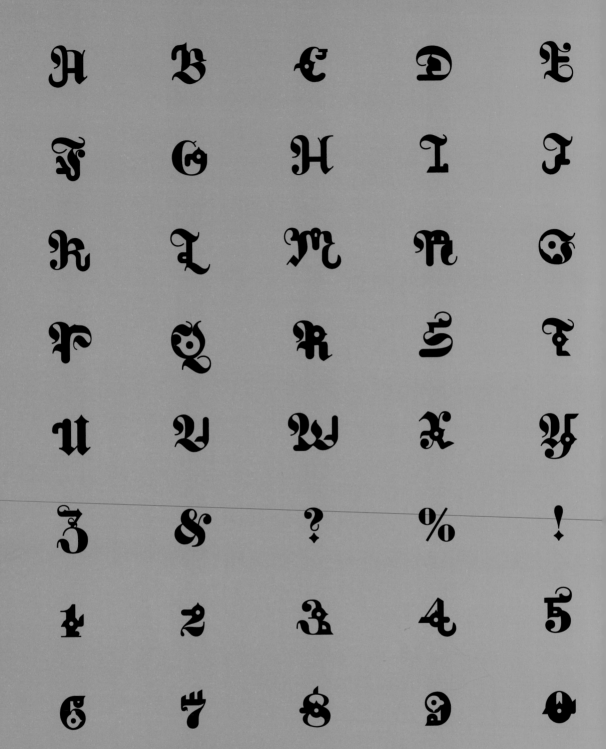

DOMINATRIX (1994)

MICHAEL WORTHINGTON

COOKIN' FONTS

Created by the designer's drag queen alter ego Francis Leatherhead, this mythical font proposes a fascistic future where cultural and personal domination occurs through language. "One world, one government, one language, one font."

14

ABCDEFGHIJKLM
NOPQRSTUVWXYZ
abcdefghijklmn
nopqrstuvwxyz
1 2 3 4 5 6 7 8 9 0

HOUSEMAID (1994)

KRISTEN FAUKNER

HOUSE INDUSTRIES

This font is based on the designer's unique illustration style which employs intricate, "slightly organic" lettering. Although it recalls the script tradition it has a novel flavor. It is, however, difficult to set and data intensive.

ABCDEFGHIJKLMNOPQRSTUVWXYZ
ABCDEFGHIJKLMNOPQRSTUVWXYZ
1234567890

AaBbCcDdEeFfGgHhIiJjKkLlMm
NnOoPpQqRrSsTtUuVvWwXxYyZz
1234567890

1234567890
ABCDEFGHIJKLMNOPQRSTUVWXYZ

ULTRABRONZO (1989)

MOURI MARUR &
RICK VALICENTI

THIRSTYPE

Originally designed for the launch of the Esse grade for Gilbert Paper Company, and used thereafter in specimen pieces, Ultrabronzo was designed to be "Copperplate meets Bank Gothic on the way to the 1990s," explain the designers.

A B C D E

F G H I J

K L M N O

P Q R S T

U V W X Y

Z & ? % !

1 2 3 4 5

6 7 8 9 0

FF STAMP GOTHIC (1992)

JUST VAN ROSSUM

FONTSHOP INTERNATIONAL

Stamp Gothic is a digital version of the designer's childhood rubber stamp set. Based on typefaces that appear in everyday life, these letters were scanned, redrawn, and perfected so that the result looks remarkably like the dirty, ephemeral originals.

EPAULET (1994)

CHRIS MACGREGOR

T-26

This script face started as a rough outline of the letters. As an accident the designer removed the curve information. He liked the effect even better than the original and let the pixels fall where they might. "From there the typeface designed itself," he says.

17

ABCDEFGHIJKLMNOPQRSTUVWXYZ
abcdefghijklmnopqrstuvwxyz
1234567890
ABCDEFGHIJKLMNOPQRSTUVWXYZ
ABCDEFGHIJKLMNOPQRSTUVWXYZ
abcdefghijklmnopqrstuvwxyz
1234567890

SEBASTIAN LESTER T-26	"Wanted for Crimes Against Banality," says the designer, who put 450 hours into making this face. The initial drawings for the font stemmed from reading *Thus Spake Zarathustra,* and the face is inspired by the mischievous character, Nietzschean.

A B C D E F G H I J K L M N O P Q R

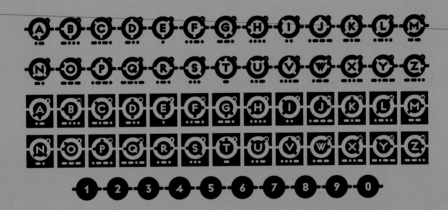

S T U V W X Y Z 1 2 3 4 5 6 7 8 9 0

FF IDENTIFICATION (1993)

RIAN HUGHES FONTSHOP INTERNATIONAL	This multicode alphabet was designed as a display face that pastes a classic sans serif in a graphic frame. Included as font variations are Morse and Semaphore. The toggle effect allows for overlays of the components.

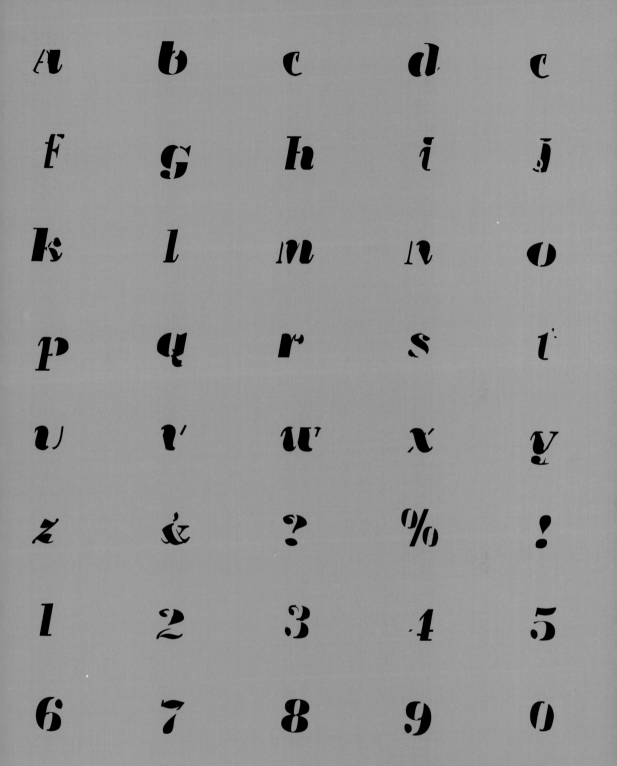

FUTILE (1993)

RODNEY SHELDON FEHSENFELD

GARAGE FONTS

Created as an italic companion to International Disgrace, with a tip of the hat to Ultra Bodoni. The lowercase letters are housed within the boundaries of its upper-case counterpart, giving it a degraded character.

A B C D E

F G H I J

K L M N O

P Q R S T

U V W X Y

Z & ? % !

1 2 3 4 5

6 7 8 9 0

SABBATH BLACK (1996)

MILES NEWLYN

EMIGRE, INC FONTS

Based on medieval Gothics, Sabbath Black evokes the look of incunabula and the logo of the *New York Times*. This version suggests more of the scribe's hand than other cuts of the historic face.

A B C D E

F G H I J

K L M N O

P Q R S T

U V W X Y

Z & ? % !

1 2 3 4 5

6 7 8 9 0

BASTARDVILLE (1994)

DAN DEWITT

DEWITT ANTHONY

Bastardville was created out of "manipulated genetic material from a rotting eighteenth-century corpse (. . . apologies to the family of Mr. John Baskerville), surgically implanted in the developing embryo during gestation," explains the designer.

A B C D E
F G H I J
K L M N O
P Q R S T
U V W X Y
Z Ç ? % !
1 2 3 4 5
6 7 8 9 0

FF KARTON (1992)

JUST VAN ROSSUM

FONTSHOP INTERNATIONAL

Fontshop calls this part of the "Ironic style category" typefaces named after the places they come from, in this case cardboard boxes. "The fonts are character sets from the world around us. We see them everyday, but do not...see the letters as typefaces."

ABCDEFGHIJKLMNOPQRSTUVWXYZ

ABCDEFGHIJKLMNOP

abcdefghijklmnopqrstuvwxyz

QRSTUVWXYZ

1234567890

ABCDEFGHIJKLMNOPQRSTUVWXYZ

abcdefghijklmnopqrstuvwxyz

abcdefghijklmnopqrstuvwxyz

1234567890

1234567890

PERSONNAGE (1996)

BRIAN HORNER

AMERICAN TYPE CORP.

Personnage is very 90s and deliberately alludes to, indeed parodies, the trends born on the West Coast that have influenced modern typography. "[A] lot of new type has this secondhand copycat look to it," says the designer.

ABCDEFGHIJKLMNOPQRSTUVWXYZ

abcdefghijklmnopqrstuvwxyz

1234567890 ABCDEFGHIJKLMNOPQRSTUVWXYZ

abcdefghijklmnopqrstuvwxyz

1234567890 ABCDEFGHIJKLMNOPQRSTUVWXYZ

abcdefghijklmnopqrstuvwxyz

1234567890

FAST GIRLS (1995)

PATRICKING

THIRSTYPE

Fast Girls grew out of the rave moment in the early nineties as it hit the rural southern United States. It also grew out of a combination of templates culled from early sketches of Futura and the "near automatic" art the designer developed for nightclubs.

THE TERM *GREEKING* DOES NOT DATE

BACK TO THE ANCIENT GREEKS. ITS

ETYMOLOGY CAN ONLY BE TRACED

AS FAR AS THE LATE NINETEENTH

CENTURY AND REFERS TO THE HAND-

DRAWN APPROXIMATION OF LINES

OF TYPE ON A ROUGH LAYOUT. COMMERCIAL

PRINTERS AND TYPOGRAPHERS SO PRECISELY

GREEKED TYPE THAT THE COMPOSITOR WAS

ABLE TO PERFECTLY DUPLICATE THE TYPE

STYLE, POINT SIZE, CHARACTER SPACING, AND

LINE LEADING.

IN THE DIGITAL WORLD TYPE NEED NOT BE

GREEKED AS IN THE EPOCH BC (BEFORE COM-

PUTERS). THE SKILLS REQUIRED FOR SUCH

PRECISION HANDLETTERING HAVE ALL BUT

ATROPHIED TODAY. BUT RECENTLY, AN

INCREASING NUMBER OF THE MOST CURIOUS

(AND INVENTIVE) NEW ALPHABETS APPEAR TO

HAVE DRAWN INSPIRATION FROM THE GREEK-

ING PROCESS. QUITE A FEW OF THESE NEW

FACES HAVE BEEN DIGITALLY DRAWN TO

SUGGEST THE HUMAN HAND.

NONE OF THE ALPHABETS IN

THIS SECTION ARE SO

FAITHFULLY COPIED FROM

OTHER ROMANS THAT THEY

CAN BE CALLED FACSIMILES,

BUT ALL HAVE ANCESTRAL

RELATIONSHIPS TO TRADITIONAL

LETTERFORMS. THE MOST

WILDLY EXPERIMENTAL TYPEFACES OWE A

DEBT TO THE CLASSICS, IF ONLY AS MODEL

FOR DEPARTURE.

ROMAN

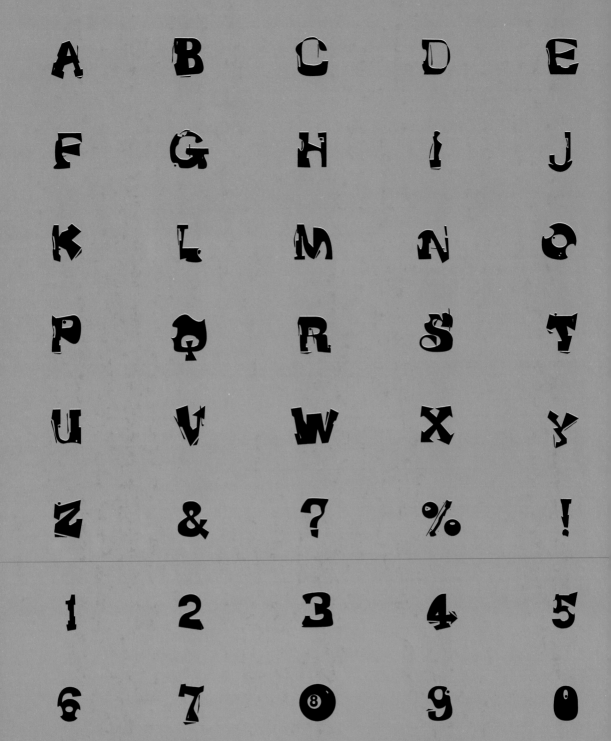

JACKASS (1996)

DOUG NOVAK

EXPLODING FONTS

The designer warns that Jackass can only be useful in "select situations." It is a headline face consistent with the trend in degradation and cut with wit. The title gives it away, but also note the numeral 8.

TEENAGER (1994)

NANCY MAZZEI &
BRIAN KELLY

GARAGE FONTS

Teenager was influenced by the Magic Marker lettering that appears on truck signs around New York City. The unpretentious nature of this lettering can never be taught in school, but it *can* be scanned into the computer and manipulated.

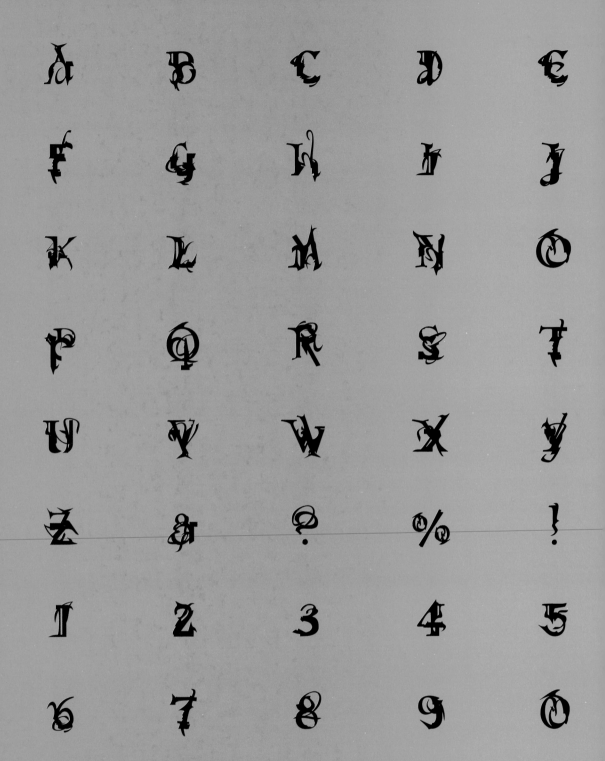

OSPREY (1993)

STEPHEN FARRELL

T-26

The montage that comprises Osprey is a patchwork of surfaces tangled in "buried history." Modeled from bits of type designs spanning 400 years, this face developed from "gothicizing" a face called Entropy, with roots in Memphis and Garamond.

ABCDEFGHIJKL
MNOPQRSTUVW
XYZabcdefghijkl
mnopqrstuvwxyz
1234567890

ABCDEFGHIJKLMNOP
QRSTUVWXYZabcdef
ghijklmnopqrstuvwxyz
1234567890

MEGA (1994)

BRIAN HORNER

AMERICAN TYPE CORP.

This face is an eclectic blend of many other novelty types, "type associated with the early days of computers to the type found in sci-fi movies." It is an homage to the retro-future look that emerges every couple of years.

ABCDEFGHIJKLMNOPQRSTUVWXYZ
abcdefghijklmnopqrstuvwxyz
1234567890

ABCDEFGHIJKLMNOPQRSTUVWXYZ
abcdefghijklmnopqrstuvwxyz
1234567890

BAUFY (1994)

BOB AUFULDISH

FONTBOY

This is a baroque version of the designer's own handwriting. Created in an academic setting, it is actually the doodles done during long committee meetings where he obsessively drew the same letter over and over. Weights range from normal to chunky.

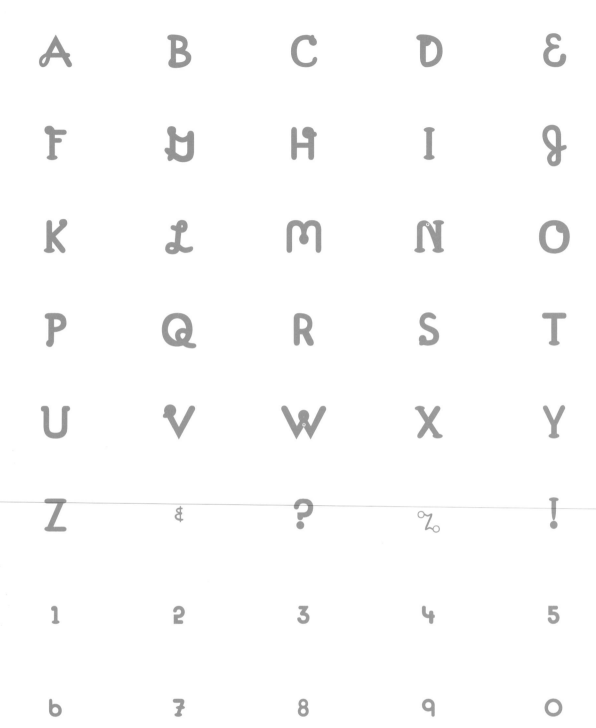

TREAT TYPE (1995)

BRIAN HORNER

AMERICAN TYPE CORP.

Treat Type is the kind of writing one might find in a 12-year-old girl's diary. It is not a literal translation but rather a tribute to the naïve, funky, and off beat. The designer also wanted to keep it very "modern and hip."

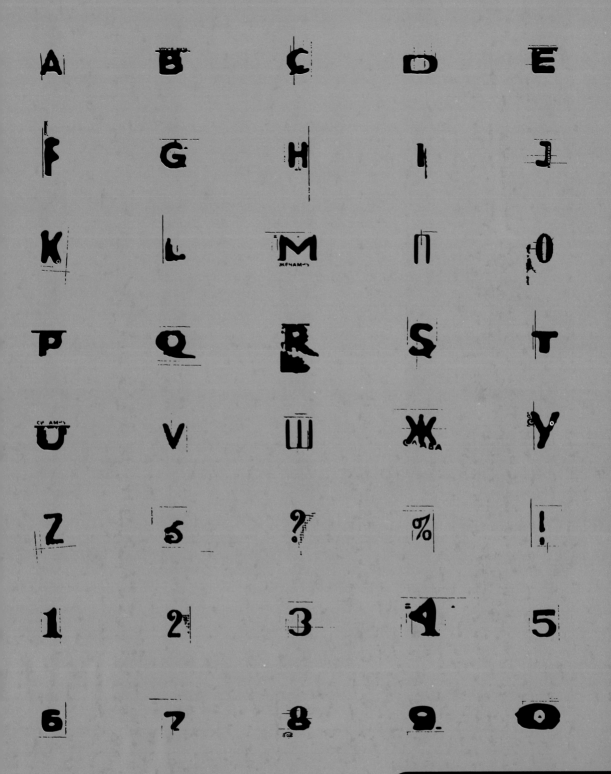

GLUE (1996)

JIM MARCUS

T-26

Surprisingly, this face is based on scans of various wood type letters, which the designer then redrew. When he ran out of letters he made his own, forming hybrids from the originals. With Glue it is possible to create very complex messes, easily.

ABCDEFGHIJKLMNOPQRSTUVWXYZ

abcdefghijklmnopqrstuvwxyz

ABCDEFGHIJKLMNOPQRSTUVWXYZ

1234567890

abcdefghijklmnopqrstuvwxyz

ABCDEFGHIJKLMNOPQRSTUVWXYZ

1234567890

abcdefghijklmnopqrstuvwxyz

1234567890

DROPLET (1992)

HAT NGUYEN T-26	Droplet's fluid characteristics suggest an organic quality of nature. The designer tried to "capture and express the aquatic emotion with all its forms and dimensions." He looked back upon his childhood in Vietnam when he played in the rain for hours.

ABCDEFGHIJKLMNOPQRSTUVWXYZ

ABCDEFGHIJKLMNOPQRSTUVWXYZ

ABCDEFGHIJKLMNOPQRSTUVWXYZ

abcdefghijklmnopqrstuvwxyz

abcdefghijklmnopqrstuvwxyz

abcdefghijklmnopqrstuvwxyz

1234567890

1234567890

1234567890

DERISION (1995)

DON SYNSTELIEN PLAZM FONTS	This face began with Aspersion and was sold through his own foundry, SynFonts. The inspiration came from playing with bitmapped fonts in Photoshop and trying to develop a visual statement that implied computer generation and human imperfection.

SPIN (1994)

CHARLES WILKIN

PROTOTYPE

Spin is a collection of elements inspired by handwritten manuscripts, blackletter scripts, and Gothic-style faces that predate the invention of movable type. Simple shapes and ornamental serifs define this "post modern manuscript" face.

TOBIAS FRERE-JONES

UNRELEASED

This is an exploration into how reading is taught. "We see letterforms every day that bear little resemblance to what we saw as children," notes the designer. To test the nature of perception these characters both approximate convention and use confusing forms.

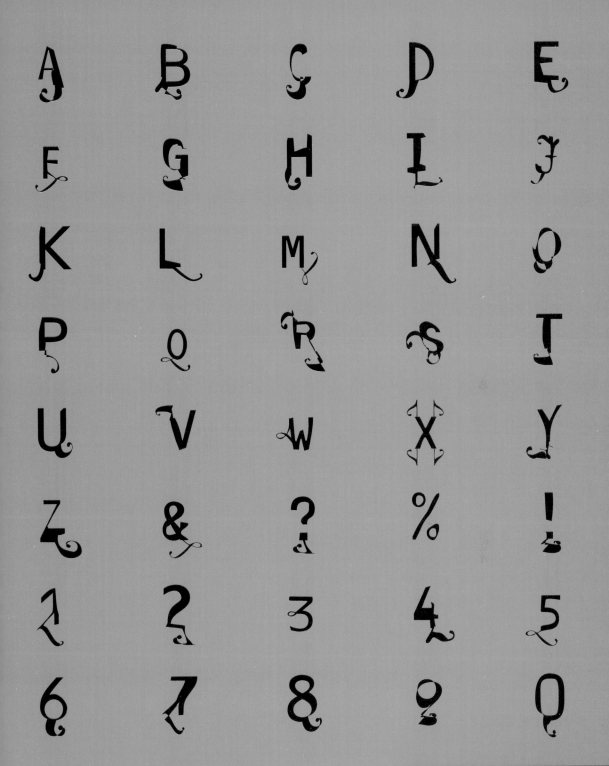

"Photosynthetic growth and heliotropic form," the designer writes about his invention. "Pure scientific method. Fungus-like bacteriological response to impaired cognitive process. . . . I think of mushrooms, warriors in the nature/culture debate."

DYSPHASIA (1993)

ELLIOT EARLS

THE APOLLO PROGRAM

AbCdEFGhiJKLMNOPQRSTUVWXYZ
AbCdEFGhiJKLMNOPQRSTUVWXYZ
1234567890
1234567890

AbCdEFGhiJKLMNOPQRSTUVWXYZ
AbCdEFGhiJKLMNOPQRSTUVWXYZ
1234567890
1234567890

AbCdEFGhiJKLMNOPQRSTUVWXYZ
AbCdEFGhiJKLMNOPQRSTUVWXYZ
1234567890
1234567890

WIT (1995)

PAUL SYCH

THIRSTYPE

Wit is an adaptation of Kurt Schwitters's 1927 alphabet. The designer was "outraged" by Schwitters' use of larger vowels. In wit, a simpler use of larger vowels was employed to give the font a quality of imbalance.

ABCDEFGHIJKLMNOPQRSTUVWXYZ
ABCDEFGHIJKLMNOPQRSTUVWXYZ
1234567890 ABCDEFGHIJKLMNOPQRSTUVWXYZ
ABCDEFGHIJKLMNOPQRSTUVWXYZ
ABCDEFGHIJKLMNOPQRSTUVWXYZ 1234567890
ABCDEFGHIJKLMNOPQRSTUVWXYZ
1234567890

D 44 (1994)

FABRIZIO SCHIARI

T-26

D44 is a "blown out" deconstructivist face. The inspiration comes from graffiti found in Honduras. D44's emphasis is on the basic shape of the letters and not on the details. Shapes lead to recognition. This is therefore an exercise in recognition.

JIM MARCUS

T-26

Aerator was the offspring of a font named Slide. It was designed to print quickly and used the bare minimum of points to express each glyph. The designer wanted Aerator and his other faces, Oscillator and Generator, to be used together as text and headline types.

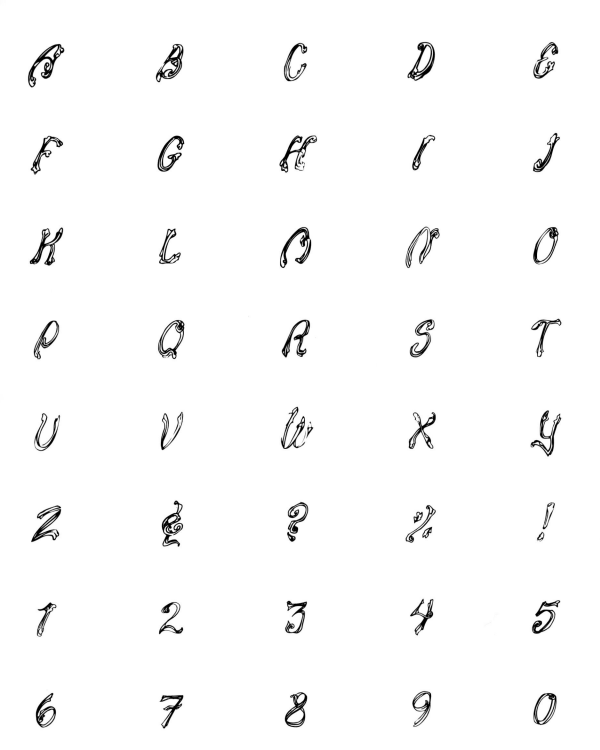

FLOREM LACTIS (1996)

SAMANTHA STAR COLE

EXPLODING FONTS

Samantha Cole builds birdcages and dressers and paints furniture and 3D art. Diesel invited her to draw an alphabet based on her art, and Florem Lactis was the first thing that popped out of her pencil." The title means *flower of the milk*.

DIGITAL

THE INSCRIPTIONAL CHARACTERS AT THE BASE OF THE TRAJAN COLUMN (ERECTED IN AD 114) IS THE HOLY GRAIL OF TRADITIONAL TYPOGRAPHY. IN 1598 M.A. ROSSI USED THESE CARVED INSCRIPTIONS AS THE MODEL FOR THE GEOMETRIC CONSTRUCTIONS THAT SET STANDARDS OF BALANCE AND PROPORTION FOR ALL ROMAN CAPITALS. DURING THE ALMOST TWO THOUSAND YEARS SINCE THIS, ONE OF THE EARLIEST KNOWN CARVINGS OF ROMAN LETTERFORMS—THE TRAJAN LETTERFORMS—HAVE BEEN SCRUTINIZED AND ANALYZED, TRACED AND REDRAWN BY TYPE DESIGNERS. PRECISE MECHANICAL SYSTEMS HAVE BEEN DEVELOPED FOR RECREATING THIS IDEAL FORM. YET DESPITE REVERENCE TO THE TRAJAN MODEL, EVEN A DEVOUT TRADITIONALIST LIKE STANLEY MORISON (THE DESIGNER OF TIMES

ROMAN) OBSERVED BACK IN THE 1930S THAT CONSTRUCTED LETTERS OFTEN SUFFER FROM THE MONOTONY OF IMITATION: "LETTERFORMS MAY WELL BEGIN WITH GEOMETRY, BUT ONLY THE SOVEREIGNTY OF THE EYE AND HAND CAN TRANSMUTE A DIAGRAM INTO A WORK OF ART."

KNOWINGLY OR NOT, CONTEMPORARY DESIGNERS HAVE TAKEN MORISON'S WORDS TO HEART. THE NEW DIGITAL CARVINGS ARE BY NO MEANS CONSTRAINED BY IMMUTABLE CONSTRUCTIONS BUT THRIVE ON AND REVEL IN MUTABILITY. ALTHOUGH THE TIME-HON-ORED PRECEPTS OF TYPE SHOULD NEVER BE REJECTED, NEW MEDIA NONETHELESS INSPIRE NEW METHODS AND DESIGNS. CONTEMPORARY CARVINGS ARE NOT SET IN STONE BUT IN THE PLACTICITY OF THE COMPUTER

CARVINGS

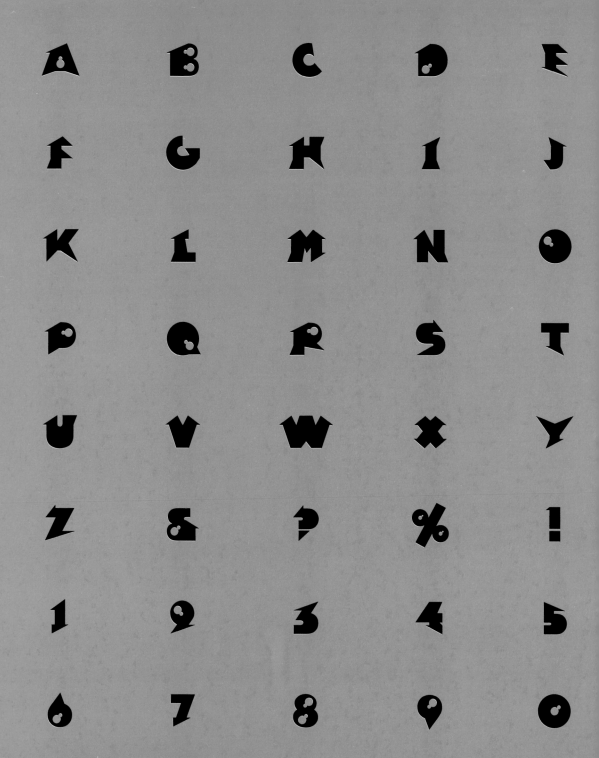

Deliberate encasing of the lowercase letterforms with the uppercase figures pro-
vides an ornamental pattern of heavy stature, influenced by architecture of the era
reflected in the name of the typeface.

ABCDEFGHIJKLMN

0123456789

OPQRSTUVWXYZ

ZYXWVUTSRQP

1234567890

ONMLKJIHGFEDCBA

BOXSPRING & MATTRESS (1994)

CARLOS SEGURA &
SCOTT SMITH

T-26

Based on an old typeface seen on certain flea market antiques, Boxspring came before Mattress. The designers redrew the samples, and after it was finished found to their surprise that it was an existing font. Mattress was based on Boxspring but completely redrawn into a new form.

ABCDEFGHIJKLMNOPQRSTUVWXYZ
abcdefghijklmnopqrstuvwxyz
1234567890

ABCDEFGHIJKLMNOPQRSTUVWXYZ
abcdefghijklmnopqrstuvwxyz
1234567890

ABCDEFGHIJKLMNOPQRSTUVWXYZ
abcdefghijklmnopqrstuvwxyz
1234567890

DOGMA (1995)

ZUSANA LICKO

EMIGRE FONTS

Dogma comes in three styles. It echos earlier twentieth-century letters—Futura, Peignot—yet is decidedly a contemporary face. Dogma Outline recalls the outline displays so popular in the sixties, but its bold curvilinearity is totally of its time.

A B C D E

F G H I J

K L M N O

P Q R S T

U V W X Y

Z & ? % !

1 2 3 4 5

6 7 8 9 0

KEEDY SANS (1989)

JEFFERY KEEDY

EMIGRE FONTS

This was loosely based on Highway Gothic, the typeface used on highway signage in America. The designer wanted a typeface with the same quirky vernacular crudeness but added "the idea of irregularity and systematic inconsistency."

44

A   B   C   D   E

F   G   H   I   J

K   L   M   N   O

P   Q   R   S   T

U   V   W   X   Y

Z   &   ?   %   !

1   2   3   4   5

6   7   8   9   0

HERNIA

ELLIOT EARLS

THE APOLLO PROGRAM

"Like a sprained ankle or torn cornea, the designer strove for the kinesthetic in type design. "Armature and musculature" is the way he describes this odd concoction. More a sculptural work than a typeface, Hernia suggests the ancient engravings."

ABCDEFGHIJKLMNOPQRSTUVWXYZ
ABCDEFGHIJKLMNOPQRSTUVWXYZ
ABCDEFGHIJKLMNOPQRSTUVWXYZ
1234567890
1234567890
1234567890
abcdefghijklmnopqrstuvwxyz
abcdefghijklmnopqrstuvwxyz
abcdefghijklmnopqrstuvwxyz

KOOKOO (1994)

MICHAEL WORTHINGTON

COOKIN' FONTS

Created as a text font for London's *Mute* magazine, KooKoo was reworked into a "dysfunctional" typographic family comprised of Bloater, Fatboy, and Bulimic. "These fonts ran away from their real families and found adopted bliss," the designer explains.

ABCDEFGHIJKLMNOPQRSTUVWXYZ
abcdefghijklmnopqrstuvwxyz
1234567890
ABCDEFGHIJKLMNOPQRSTUVWXYZ
abcdefghijklmnopqrstuvwxyz
1234567890
ABCDEFGHIJKLMNOPQRSTUVWXYZ
abcdefghijklmnopqrstuvwxyz
1234567890

BAUKASTEŃ (1995)

ALESSIO LEONARDI

FONTSHOP INTERNATIONAL

This face and its various weights are constructed with building blocks of several colors. More a typographic game than a typeface, it exaggerates the bitmapped look and it gives new meaning to the phrase obsessive-compulsive.

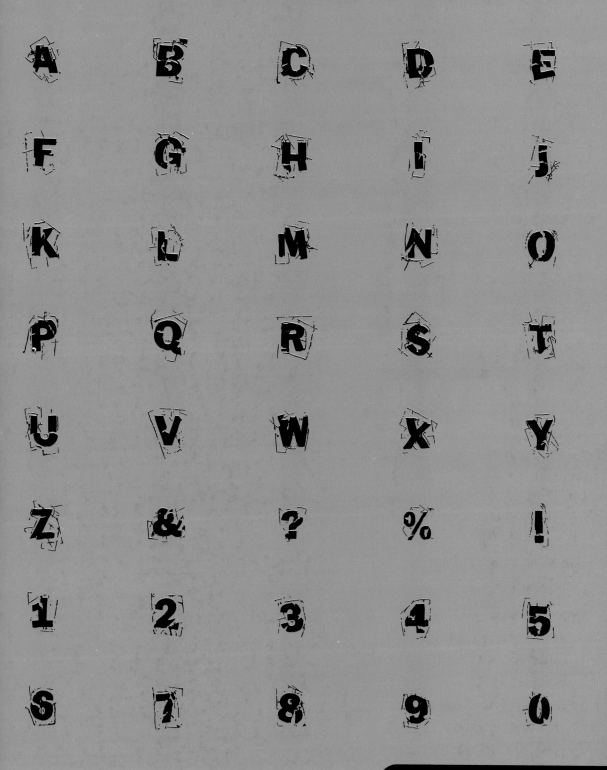

HOUSEARREST (1995)

JEREMY DEAN

HOUSE INDUSTRIES

Housearrest is based on what transfer type would look like it if was taped down to a surface and lifted up several times. This was a difficult type to make because the adhesive-tape marks created millions of data points that had to be digitally cleaned.

A B C D E

F G H I J

K L M N O

P Q R S T

U V W X Y

Z & ? % !

1 2 3 4 5

6 7 8 9 0

TEMPLATE GOTHIC (1990)

BARRY DECK

EMIGRE FONTS

This is the quintessential digital homage to the vernacular. "There was a sign in the Laundromat where I do my laundry," the designer explains. "The sign was done with lettering templates and it was exquisite." The result is a face that looks as if it has suffered the ravages of photomechanical reproduction.

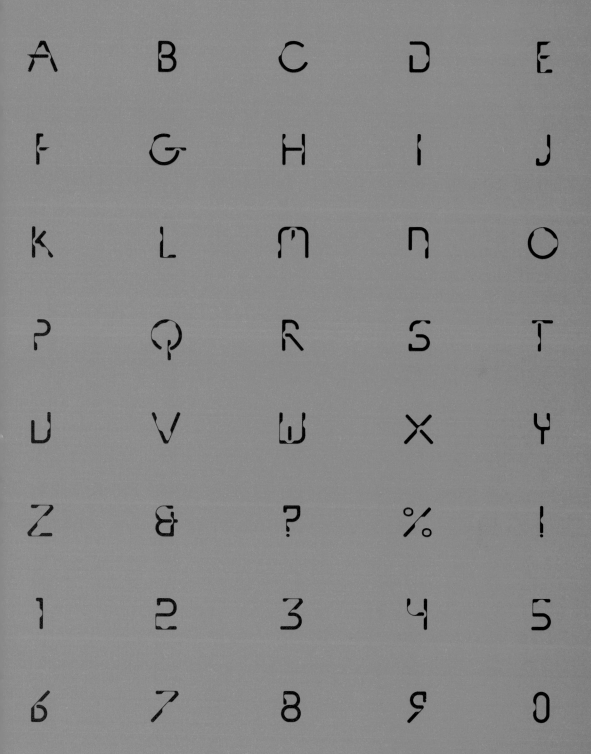

TECHNO ORGANIC (1995)

MATT HEXIMER

GARAGE FONTS

This experimental typeface combines various cliché typographic elements. The original intention of the project was to instill a distressed feel upon the letterforms similar to the effects of corrosion. An attempt was made to combine organic with sterile elements.

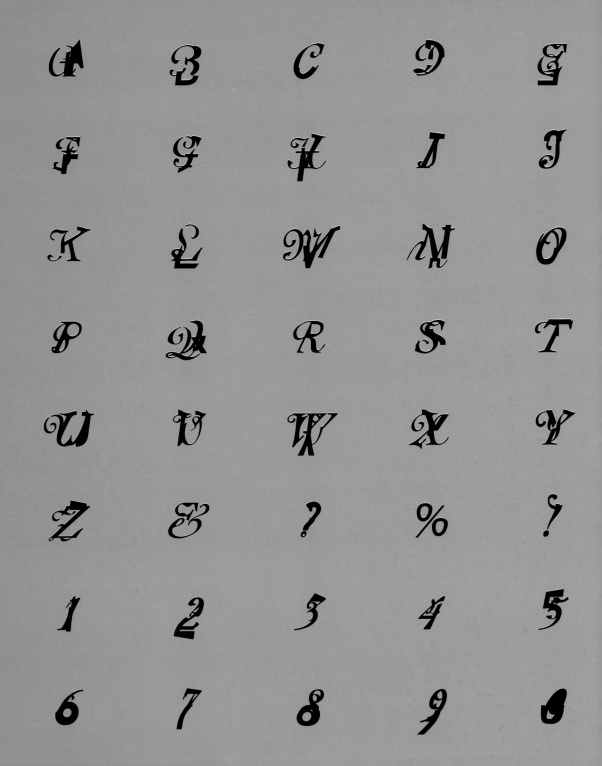

ELLIOT EARLS

THE APOLLO PROGRAM

"In high school I dated this girl," notes the designer. "She wore heavy blue eye shadow. Her eyes were brown. I hated blue eye shadow. I hate this typeface. But I liked the girl." Like the girl, the face has a curious beauty.

ABCDEFGHIJKLMNOPQRSTUVWXYZ
abcdefGhijklmnopqrstuvwxyz
1234567890
abcdefGhijklmnopqr
stuvwxyz1234567890
abcdefGhijklmnopqrstuvwxyz
abcdefGhijklmnopqrstuvwxyz
1234567890

INTERNATIONAL DISGRACE (1992)

RODNEY SHELDEN FEHSENFELD

GARAGE FONTS

This face takes a typeface like Helvetica, which is held in high esteem in the type world, and transforms it into a font to be held an international disgrace. Good, bad, different . . . . in the end, such judgment is in the eye of the user.

ABCDEFGHIJKLMNOPQR

ABCDEFGHIJKL
MNOPQRS+UVWXYZ
1234567890
S+UVWXYZ1234567890

EXOCET (1994)

JONATHAN BARNBROOK

EMIGRE FONTS

Exocet is based on primitive Greek stone carving and continues an ancient tradition. "Is type carved in stone more 'real' than a photograph of type?" asks the designer. It certainly required much more physical effort than design in the Macintosh.

A B C D E

F G H I J

K L M N O

P Q R S T

U V W X Y

Z & ? ? !

1 2 3 4 5

6 7 8 9 0

LUNATIX (1988)

ZUZANA LICKO

EMIGRE FONTS

1985 saw the launch of Emigre, the foundry's first bitmapped face. Lunatix is one of the earliest sans-bitmap digital faces to appear. It cleverly combines bitmapping and curves, suggesting a transitional letterform. And it holds up almost a decade after its release.

FETISH NO. 338 (1994-96)

JONATHAN HOEFLER

THE HOEFLER TYPE FOUNDRY

This typeface is a commentary on the classical idiom. It quotes Gothic, Victorian, Moorish, Coptic, Celtic, and Byzantine, but it is a total invention. It parodies notions of "fanciness" in which not only professional designers but the lay public hold so dear.

TRANS (1994)

JOSHUA DISTLER	Inspired by shipping labels, tracking tags, and bar codes, Trans represents a digital language spoken between computers used to manage the transport of freight. Trans comes in a variety of forms: Trans:Neg, Trans:Norm, Trans:Raw, and Trans:Extra.
SHIFT	

HTF GESTALT (1990)

JONATHAN HOEFLER	Gestalt psychology proposes that nothing is comprehensible out of its context. Similarly, a theory of legibility suggests that words are identified not by the order of their letters but by thier overall shape. Most of this face is ambiguous out of context.
THE HOEFLER TYPE FOUNDRY	

A B C D E

F G H I J

K L M N O

P Q R S T

U V W X Y

Z S ? % !

1 2 3 4 5

6 7 8 9 0

HEIMLICH MANEUVER (1994)

ELLIOT EARLS

THE APOLLO PROGRAM

This is another type-is-stranger-than-fiction face. "Select from the 'special' menu," demands the designer. "Put the typeface on a poster and charge money for them. Value? Reminds me of Barnum: 'There's a sucker born every minute.'"

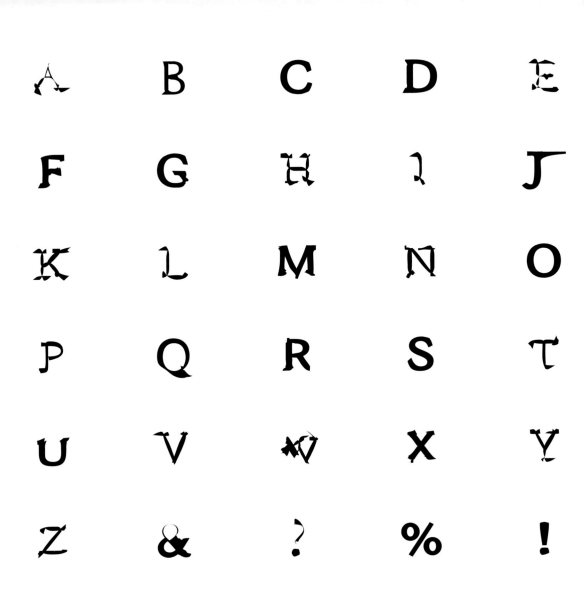

KLIEGLIGHT (1994)

ELLIOT EARLS

THE APOLLO PROGRAM

Type as a play on words. This is one of the designer's attempts to make "William Morris roll over headlong in his grave." Type that is ripped from its moorings "like the *Pequod*." It has become the signature of the designer himself.

56

A B C D E
F G H I J
K L M N O
P Q R S T
U V W X Y
Z & ? % !
1 2 3 4 5
6 7 8 9 0

DEAD HISTORY (1990)

P. SCOTT MAKELA

EMIGRE FONTS

This type signals the end of an era of traditionally produced fonts. It personifies a new attitude marked by the design of hybrid typefaces, the result of the computer's ability to function as an assembling tool. It was eventually redrawn and completed by Zuzana Licko.

A B C D E
F G H I J
K L M N O
P Q R S T
U V W X Y
Z & ? % !
1 2 3 4 5
6 7 8 9 0

TOTALLY GLYPHIC (1990)

ZUZANA LICKO

EMIGRE FONTS

Two hundred years ago black letter was as legible as Helvetica is today. Totally Glyphic is a contemporary interpretation of the oldest, most legible types in the historical archive. Although it has a medieval aura, it is totally contemporary.

ABCDEFGHIJKLMNOPQRSTUVWXYZ
abcdefghijklmnopqrstuvwxyz
1234567890

ABCDEFGHIJKLMNOPQRSTUVWXYZ
1234567890

ABCDEFGHIJKLMNOPQRSTUVWXYZ
abcdefghijklmnopqrstuvwxyz
1234567890

GREEN TERROR (1995)

ERIC LIN

T-26

Green Terror is the result of an intended transformation of natural forms—physical and chemical. Like the scientist in the movie *The Fly*, Green Terror, says the designer, is about the fear of being replaced—a sense of flirting with death.

FLYTRAP (1995)

MARCUS BURLILE

PLAZM FONTS

The inspiration for this "organic and Gothic letterform" comes from combining the visual construction of the venus flytrap plant with lost appendages of insect prey. Reduced as text, the face recalls incunabula.

JONATHAN HOEFLER

THE HOEFLER TYPE FOUNDRY

This face is an endeavor to reconcile the designer's critical and aesthetic ideas. Typefaces that reveal critical concepts have more artistic merit than those that are simply attractive, he says. But he also subscribes to a system of venerable principles.

A   B   C   D   E

F   G   H   I   J

K   L   M   N   O

P   Q   R   S   T

U   V   W   X   Y

Z   &   ?   %   !

1   2   3   4   5

6   7   8   9   0

DEMOCRATICA BOLD (1991)

"Democratia is a synthesis of the connections I saw between the crude struggle for democracy in the former USSR and the crudeness of the many recent modular typefaces," writes the designer. This font is designed with letters that suggest freedom from the old rules of typography.

MILES NEWLYN

EMIGRE FONTS

A B C D E F G H I J K L M N O P Q R S T U V W X Y Z

a b c d e f g h i j k l m n o p q r s t u v w x y z

a b c d e f g h i j k l m n o p q r s t u v w x y z

A B C D E F G H I J K L M N O P Q R S T U V W X Y Z

1 2 3 4 5 6 7 8 9 0

DISTILLATION (1995)

ELLIOT EARLS

THE APOLLO PROGRAM

"Corn mush, coiled copper tube, and a big pot," is how the designer explains this one. But this quirky font of inverted letters, with intermitent swashes for accent, is as classical as a weird digital letterform can be. Not right for all occassions, but a fine parody.

A B C D E F G H I J K L M
A B C D E F G H I J K L M
N O P Q R S T U V W X Y Z
N O P Q R S T U V W X Y Z
a b c d e f g h i j k l m n
a b c d e f g h i j k l m n
o p q r s t u v w x y z
o p q r s t u v w x y z
1 2 3 4 5 6 7 8 9 0
1 2 3 4 5 6 7 8 9 0

SUBURBAN (1993)

RUDY VANDERLANS

EMIGRE FONTS

This was the designer's first complete typeface. His goal was to incorporate into one design all of the components from hand-lettered script faces. But many of the forms were simplified and many script features stylized. The final is fairly rational, with a calligraphic touch.

A B C D E
F G H I J
K L M N O
P Q R S T
U V W X Y
Z & ? % !
1 2 3 4 5
6 7 8 9 0

MOTIVE (1995)

STEFAN HÄGERLING

FONTSHOP INTERNATIONAL

This face, says the designer, with its soluble forms can be seen as a mirror of our ever-changing society. Or as an element of pure creation. A form of plasticity can be obtained by layering different weights of FF Motive over one another.

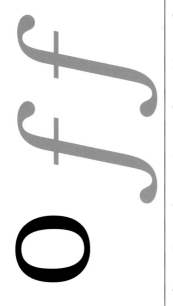

THE TERM *FACES ON THE EDGE* IMPLIES A LEVEL OF ECCENTRICITY. BUT EVEN WITHIN THIS CONTEXT SOME FACES ARE WEIRDER THAN OTHERS. THE STANDARD FOR STRANGE MUST BE JUDGED AGAINST OTHER FACES. "AROUND 1816 CASLON, IN AN EFFORT TO BE DIFFERENT, TOOK THE SERIFS OFF AND MADE A SANS SERIF TYPE WHICH WAS ULTIMATELY REJECTED," NOTES DAN SOLO, A TYPOGRAPHER WHO SPECIALIZES IN TURN-OF-THE-CENTURY ODDITIES. LATER THAT CENTURY, TYPE CRITICS ASSAILED TUSCANS, A GENRE OF DECORATIVE WOOD AND METAL TYPE WITH BIFURCATED SERIFS, AS MONSTROSITIES. THESE TYPES WERE TOO WEIRD FOR THE TRADI-TIONALISTS, BUT VERY POPULAR AMONG THE MASSES. OFF THE WALL FOR ONE MIGHT BE HUNG ON THE WALL AS ANOTHER'S ART.

LIMIT-TESTING IS NOT THE CRITE-

RION FOR INCLUSION IN THIS SECTION.

THESE FACES FIT INTO TWO SEPARATE

BUT OFTEN INTERSECTING CATEGORIES:

(1). THOSE DERIVED FROM THE STREET

OR WALLS (I.E., COMMON VISUAL DETRITUS

LIKE STORE SIGNS, BILLBOARDS, COFFEE CUPS)

AND (2). THOSE THAT ARE METAPHORICALLY

OFF THE WALL, IN THE SENSE OF NOT FITTING

INTO ANY PRECONCEIVED NOTION OF HOW AND

WHY TYPE IS DESIGNED.

TYPE AS ART? THIS IS THE NEXUS BETWEEN

EXPRESSION AND FUNCTIONALITY WHERE

EVEN SEEMINGLY DEMENTED FACES FUNCTION

BEYOND THE INTENT OF THEIR CREATOR IN THE

HANDS OF A DESIGNER WITH A MORE ABSURD

VISION.

THE *a* LL

A B C D E
P G H I J
K L M N O
P Q R S T
U V W X Y
Z ¢ ? % !
1 2 3 4 5
6 7 8 9 0

ROUNDHOUSE (1995)

ALLEN MERCER

HOUSE INDUSTRIES

Inspired by the looseness of a lunatic face called Funhouse, one of this foundry's original fonts, the curvaceous Roundhouse also has roots in cartoon and comic book lettering dating back to the 1930s and 40s.

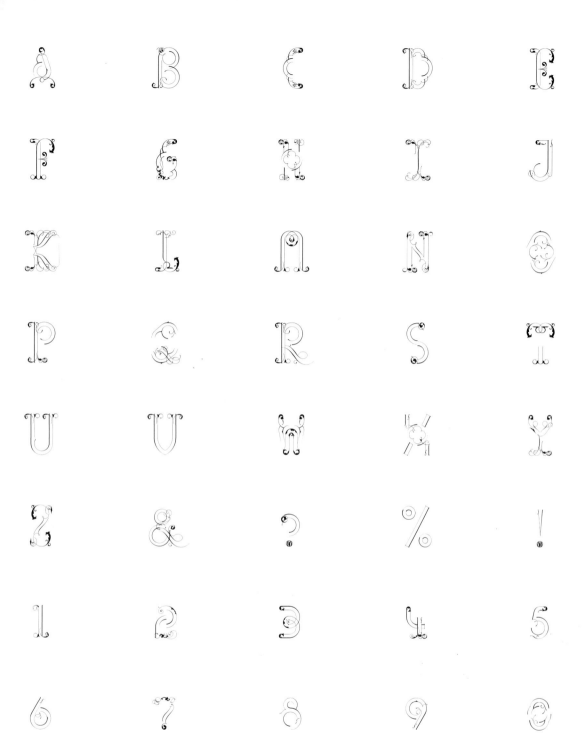

MISSIONARY (1991)

MILES NEWLYN

EMIGRE FONTS

Missionary is most similar to the vernacular lettering of the Celtic manuscripts from the period after the Romans left Britain. "This was a time when," says the designer, "new ideas and influences were being applied to the Roman alphabet."

A B C D E
F G H I J
K L M N O
P Q R S T
U V W X Y
Z & ? % !*

1 2 3 4 5
6 7 8 9 0

PETER GIRALDI

T-26

"When I began to design this face," says the designer, "I sat down with my Saul Bass titles, UPA cartoons, monster comics, and toy catalogs." It took about two weeks to draw it in pencil, then another month to digitize the font, trying to preserve the hand-lettered feel in the final version.

CHAINLETTER (1993)

TOBIAS FRERE-JONES

UNRELEASED

Based on the cumulative effects of copying on a Xerox machine, Chainletter degrades individual forms to illegibility but retains enough of the structure to function in text. When read in context it is perfectly legible.

RBCDEFGHIJKLMNOPQRSTUUWHYZ

abcderghijklmnopqrstuuwhyz

1234567890

RBCDEFGHIJKLMNOPQRSTUUWHYZ

abcderghijklmnopqrstuuwhyz

1234567890

DINK (1994)

CHARLES WILKIN

PROTOTYPE

The use of simple shapes and the interaction of those shapes created these letter-forms. The designer introduced the concept of legibility and "universal characters"—the letter u for example, is the same for both upper and lower case.

A B C D E

F G H I J

K L M N O

P Q R S T

U V W X Y

Z & ? % !

1 2 3 4 5

6 7 8 9 0

WHIZBANG (1995)

ANDRE KUZNIAREK

STUDIO DAEDALUS

Like Howard Trafton's Cartoon (1936), Whizbang is based on the hand-lettering common in comic books. On its own it is a semibold collection of capitals, but when used in comics or comic-like art it is an effective facsimile of the real thing.

Oscillator was designed as the headline for a flyer for a rave called Generator. Its parent was a font called Slide, but adjustments were made to the basic form in Illustrator, which created the slippery target look.

JIM MARCUS

T-26

71

ABCDEFGHIJKLMNOPQRSTUVWXYZ

abcdefghijklmnopqrstuvwxyz
ABCDEFGHIJKLMNOPQRSTUVWXYZ
1234567890

abcdefghijklmnopqrstuvwxyz1234567890
ABCDEFGHIJKLMNOPQRSTUVWXYZ

abcdefghijklmnopqrstuvwxyz

1234567890

BOB AUFULDISH

FONT BOY

Whiplash demonstrates the meeting of an engineer's template and a pressure-sensitive input device. The underlying structure is rational; the form resting on that structure is processed based. Whiplash Lineola uses interference to subvert the grid structure formed by monospacing.

ABCDEFGHIJKLMNOPQRSTUVWXYZ

ABCDEFGHIJKLMNOPQRSTUVWXYZ

1234567890

1234567890

ABCDEFGHIJKLMNOPQRSTUVWXYZ

ABCDEFGHIJKLMNOPQRSTUVWXYZ

BACKSPACER (1993)

NANCY MAZZEI &
BRIAN KELLEY

EMIGRE FONTS

Each key in Backspacer toys with how technically similar a character has to be in order for the entire set to be visually related. The familiar image of the keys guides the readers mind to fill in the blanks and allows each letterform to become more individual.

"Grey steel walls and taxpayer television," the designer explains as his influences for this face. "Three square meals, Jack. The grueling discipline of the process, like chain gang music, is sweet sunlight to the prisoner . . . ."

PROTON 2 (1994)

PATRICK GIASSON

T-26

The designer began working on this for a CD-ROM to commemorate the fiftieth anniversary of the bombing of Hiroshima and Nagasaki. A-bomb technology was based on molecular fission; this typeface represents the modular representation of chemical molecules by spheres and links.

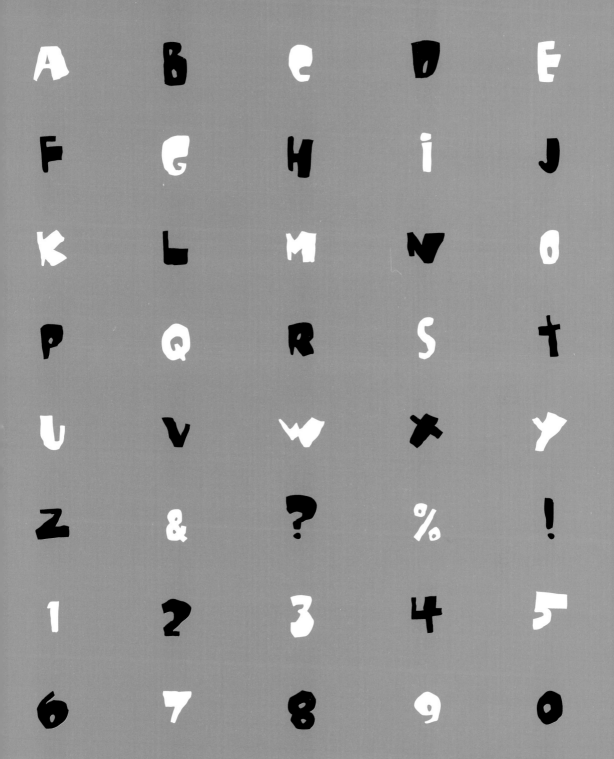

BEACHOUSE (1994)

JEREMY DEAN

HOUSE INDUSTRIES

Beachouse, an all-cap alphabet, is a simple, blocky typeface with the same charac-teristics as crude, wood-carved, expressionistic letters. The designer is known for creating distressed, rough fonts, this departure, however, emphasizes simplicity.

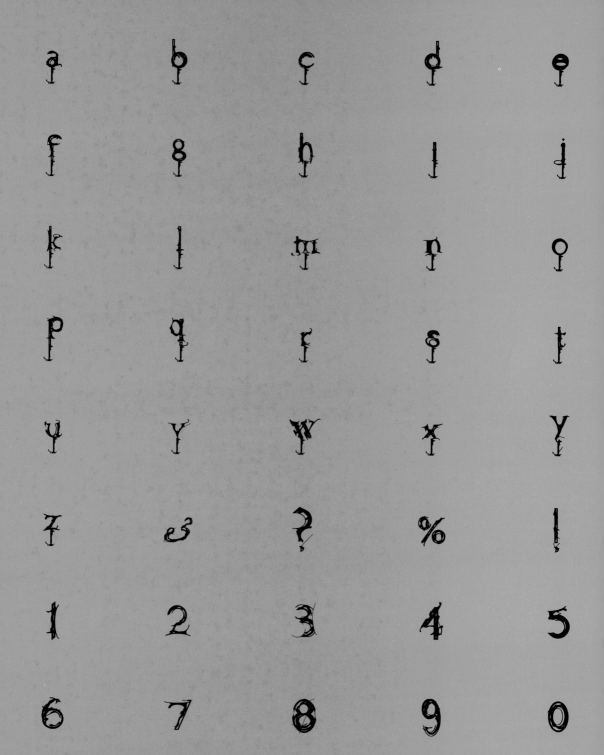

FINIAL REGULAR (1994)

JENNIFER ARTERBURY, BRAD
BRAWLEY, & NOEL CHILDS

T-26

This was designed by a design collective, built on the idea that three hands on one project, all working at the same time, was the best model. Finial was approached in the same way—each designer contributed to the font's creation by adding a personal touch to each character.

Cyberotica started life as Cyber Erotica. The designer began thick and let the computer generate thinner weights, which is in keeping with the aesthetic of the face. The name and face is definitely of its time. It was used in advertisements for Gilbert paper and soon became much sought after.

Viscosity asks the question, "Can a typeface be designed without the repetition of any individual part and still be visually unified?" One designer drew the upper case, the other the lower case. The baseline varies to help with the character fit.

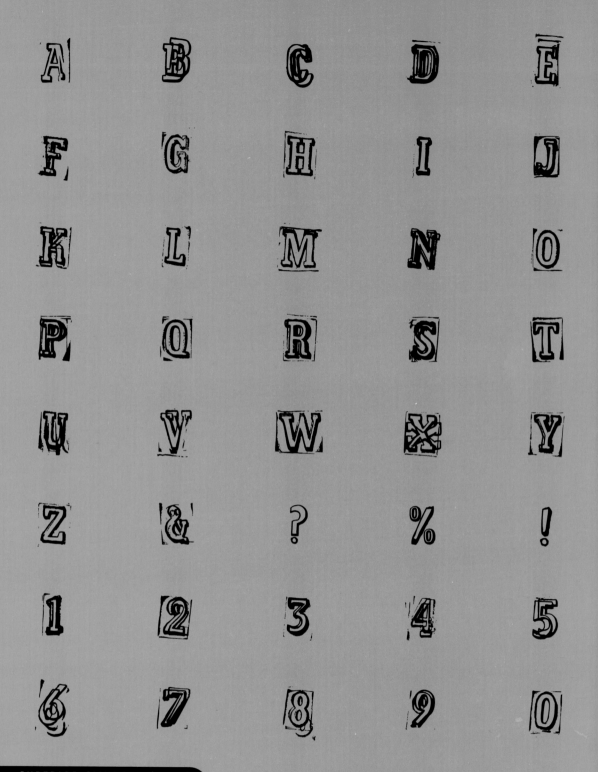

GARY HUSTWIT

T-26

These letters were derived from a set of rubber stamps from the 1930s. "I inked out the letters with varying degrees of pressure, creating the cool irregularities," the designer explains. "I completely destroyed some of the letterforms with overlaps and heavy impressions."

FAITHFUL FLY (1994)

DAVID SAGORSKI

INTERNATIONAL TYPEFACE
CORPORATION

The designer's first face, Bang, was inspired by Saturday morning cartoons from the seventies. Faithful Fly is a cross between graffiti and overstylized calligraphy, with a touch of the spiritual. Faithful suggests "godlike" and fly means "cool." The ellipses are meant to be halos.

O*ptical*

NOW YOU SEE IT, NOW YOU DON'T. NOW IT'S STATIC, NOW IT'S ERRATIC. THE COMPUTER MAKES IT SO EFFORTLESS TO TEASE THE EYE THAT TYPE DESIGNERS ARE OBLIGED TO MAKE FACES THAT SHAKE AND SHIMMY, IGNORING ALL TYPESETTING RULES. TODAY SCORES OF THESE KINETIC LETTERS FILL FOUNDRY TYPE LIBRARIES. YET WHAT IS THE VIRTUE OF DEFY- ING LEGIBILITY? SHOULD A DESIGNER MAKE A TYPEFACE THAT IS ANYTHING OTHER THAN READABLE? BUT WAIT A MINUTE. ARE THESE TYPEFACES REALLY UNREADABLE?

THE DELUSION IS THAT OPTICALLY DISTORTED TYPEFACES ARE ILLEGIBLE. DESPITE THE VISUAL NOISE AND DIGITAL DIRT SURROUNDING THEM, THEY *ARE* EASILY DECIPHERABLE; THE FUNDA- MENTAL FORM OF THE LETTERS IS INTACT.

THOUGH EMBELLISHED. LIKE SIXTIES PSYCHE-

DELIC LETTERING THAT REQUIRED READERS TO

REORIENT THEMSELVES, TODAY'S OPTICALLY

MANIPULATED DIGITAL ALPHABETS DEMAND

THAT READERS IGNORE PRECONCEPTIONS AND

FOCUS ON THE FORM. ONCE THE ADJUSTMENT IS

MADE, THE READING IS SIMPLE. THESE FONTS

ARE NOT USED FOR LONG LINES OF PROSE, THEY

ARE DISPLAY FACES THAT BOTH SYMBOLIZE

AND EMPHASIZE AN IDEA.

MANY OF THESE FACES ARE COMMENTARIES

ON TECHNOLOGY AND MODERN LIFE. DIRTY

FAX, INFLUENCED BY A TYPOGRAPHIC ERROR IN

A FAX TRANSMISSION, IS A WRY COMMENTARY

ON A NEW KIND OF VERNACULAR. AND AS THE

NAME SUGGESTS, VITRIOL IS AN ALPHABET

THAT EXPRESSES THE ANGST OF THE TIMES.

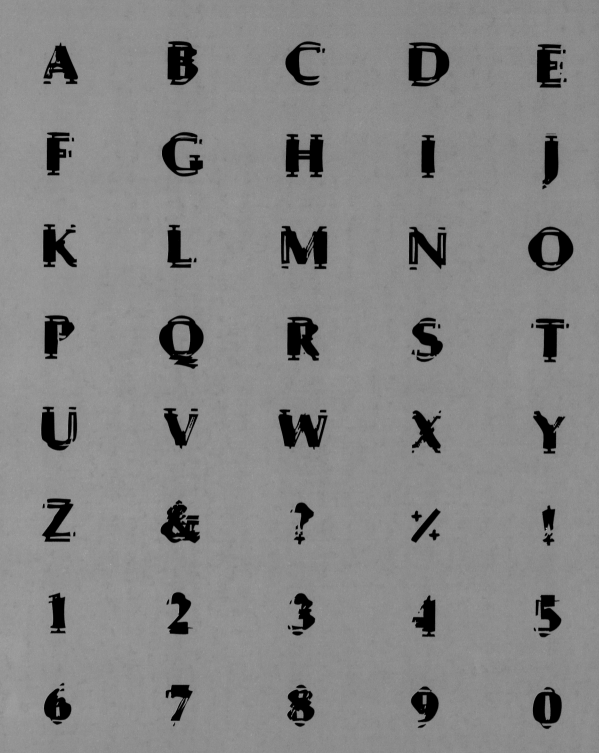

DEAN VACCARO

EXPLODING FONTS

"I didn't know what I was doing with Jitterbug until I was halfway through," the designer admits. "I had just been messing around . . . when I noticed I had accidentally made a jittery-looking alphabet. The challenge was to push it as far as I could."

ABCDEFGHIJKLMNOPQRSTUVWXYZ
ABCDEFGHIJKLMNOPQRSTUVWXYZ
abcdefghijklmnopqrstuvwxyz
abcdefghijklmnopqrstuvwxyz
et1234567890
et1234567890

ABCDEFGHIJKLMNOPQRSTUVWXYZ
ABCDEFGHIJKLMNOPQRSTUVWXYZ
abcdefghijklmnopqrstuvwxyz
abcdefghijklmnopqrstuvwxyz
et1234567890
et1234567890

INDECISION (1995)

FRANK HEINE

T-26

The motivation for another stenciled letter was to include eight different styles (plus line elements) in the Indecision family. Extensive style mixtures provide instant vitality with a strong, rough, yet workmanlike character. Word pictures are encouraged.

A A B B C C D D E E F F
G G H H I I J J K K L L M M
N N O O P P Q Q R R S S T T
U U V V W W X X Y Y Z Z

OOGA BOOGA (1993)

RICK VALICENTI &
GREG THOMPSON

THIRSTYPE

This derives from a painted sign on the side of a T-shirt factory. Photos of the sign were assigned to the least detail-conscious person at Thirstype. He scanned, traced, and stuck the letters into Fontographer. The kerning was the result of ad hoc arrangement.

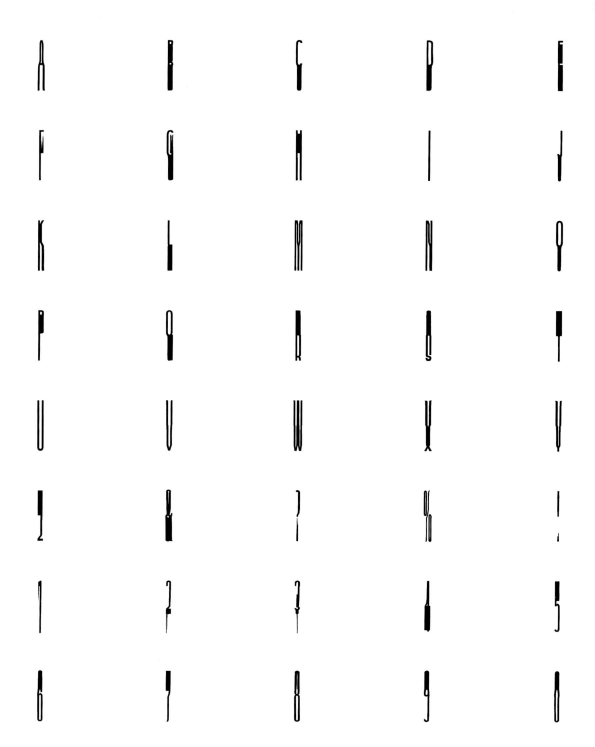

FF DIRTYFAX (1995)

FABIAN ROTTKE	The inspiration for the Regular and Heavy versions of Dirtyfax was a Xerox 7010 photocopier using heat-sensitive thermopaper. The fonts look like they got jammed in a fax machine. Although they are distorted, anyone who has had this problem will recognize the letters.
FONTSHOP INTERNATIONAL	

84

FF EKTTOR (1995)

FABIAN ROTTKE

FONTSHOP INTERNATIONAL

"I drew the letters for FF Ekttor," the designer explains," using an elderberry branch and ink." The result was an irregular set of characters from which he chose letters for each of the light and bold weights. The mixed-weight combinations are key to these characters.

ABCDEFGHIJKLMNOPQRSTUVWXYZ

aAbBcCdDeEfFgGhHiIjJkK

lLmMnNoOpPqQrRsStTuU

vVuWxXyYzZ&1234567890

ABCDEFGHIJKLMNOPQRSTUVWXYZ

OCCIDENTAL DISMOUNT (1993)

RODNEY SHELDEN FEHSENFELD

THIRSTYPE

This was an exercise in creating a character set of letterforms using three basic components—short stems, long stems, and ovals. It projects an ad hoc look but in fact is a very rational collection of related typographic forms.

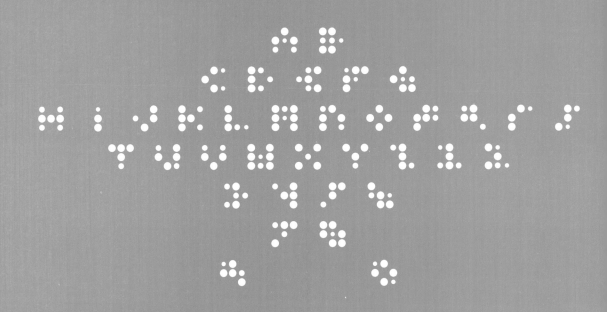

ALIEN:GREY (1995)

JOSHUA DISTLER

SHIFT

Alien:Grey was produced as an experiment in the use of minimal elements. What precipitated it was a 3 x 3 matrix made up of three different dot sizes. The matrix functions on a textural level at large sizes and conveys a gray tone at smaller sizes where the dots optically merge together.

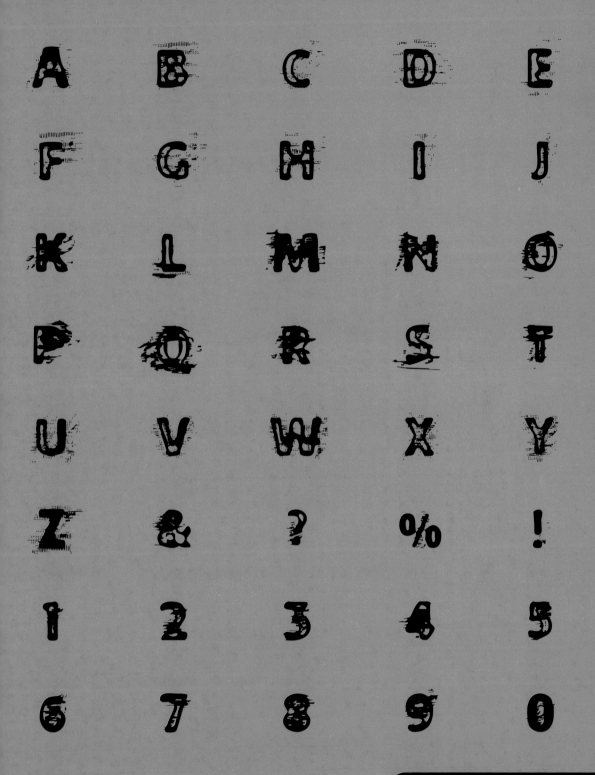

PULSITALIA (1995)

DAVE HENDERLIETER

PLAZM FONTS

The designer admits that this face was inspired by a concussion he received from a car accident. "I woke up and was staring at the lettering on the door of a tow truck, seeing quite a bit of haze and streaks around everything." This is a recreation of those letters.

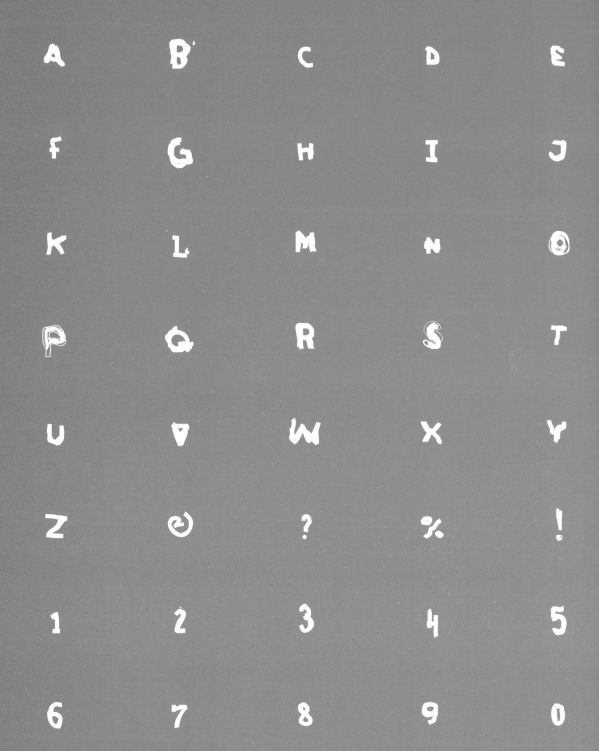

FABRIZIO SCHIAVI

FONTSHOP INTERNATIONAL

The assonance in the drawing of FF GeäbOil matches the assonance of grunge music. The user's eye perceives sensations like the ear captures sensations from a song without words. The characters are often indefinable objects. They are chosen for their "sonic weight."

CASSANDRA

TOBIAS FRERE-JONES

UNRELEASED

Cassandra was an attempt to "tamper with the recipe of character structure while pre-serving the ingredients." Garage Gothic was split horizontally and the top and bot-tom fragments switched. With zero leading, the half characters recombine into new characters. Gestalt principles collided head-on, with the reader as the first casualty.

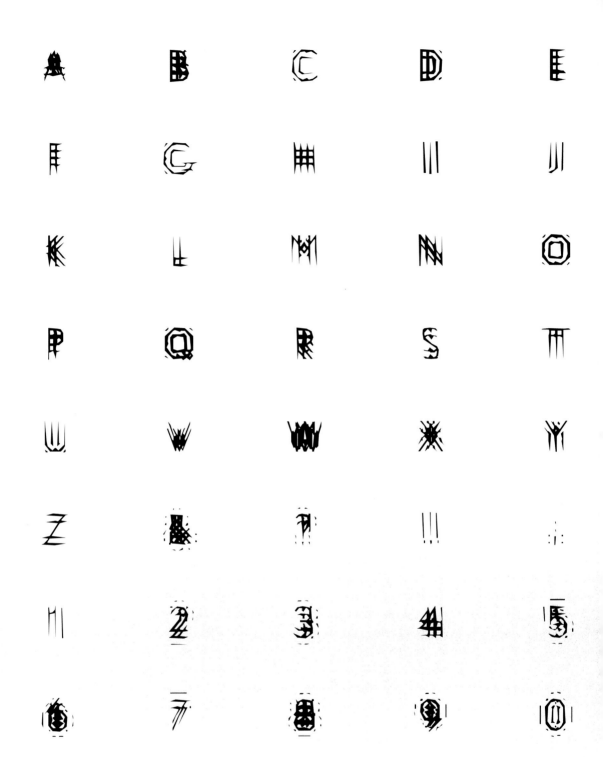

TOBIAS FRERE-JONES

UNRELEASED

If an H is two verticals and a horizontal, would a character with four verticals and three horizontals really be an H? The characters of Nobel Light were made to feed back on themselves. This noise both obscures and reinforces the identities of the letters.

ABCDEFGHIJKLMNOPQRSTUVWXYZ

abcdefghijklmnopqrstuvwxyz

1234567890

& &

1234567890

abcdefghijklmnopqrstuvwxyz

ABCDEFGHIJKLMNOPQRSTUVWXYZ

MITTEN (1996)

CHRIS MACGREGOR

T-26

The inspiration for this comes from all the "free kitten" and "lemonade" signs nailed to electric poles. The designer calls these 3D shapes "jello letters." "I wanted Mitten to reflect the unpracticed hand that makes up most people's first experience of graphic design."

AaBbCcDdEe AaBbCcDdEe
AaBbCcDdEeFf
FfGgHhIiJjKk FfGgHhIiJjKk
GgHhIiJjKkLlM
LlMmNnOoPp LlMmNnOoPp
MmNnOoPpQqRrSs
QqRrSsTtUu QqRrSsTtUu
TtUuVvWwXxYy
VvWwXxYyZz VvWwXxYyZz
ZzG1234567890
G1234567890 G1234567890

NARLY (1993)

ZUZANA LICKO

EMIGRE FONTS

Cloud-like in its gnarled form, this family of faces pushes the ability of digital technology to do what the hand wants. Narly is is built from overlapping curlicue dots. These are then fused and outlined in various ways to form five mutations.

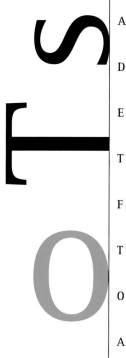

A PRINTER'S FLOWER, JEWEL, OR DINGBAT IS A DECORATIVE DEVICE USED TO ADD COLOR AND EMPHASIS. THROUGHOUT TYPE HISTORY THESE TYPOGRAPHIC BITS WERE FOUNDED IN FORMS FROM ABSTRACT GLYPHS TO MINICARTOONS. IN THE DIGITAL AGE—ALSO KNOWN AS THE EPOCH OF LITTLE ICONS—THE WITTY DINGBAT ENJOYS A SERIOUS REVIVAL.

JUST THE WORD *DINGBAT* SUGGESTS SOME-THING A WEE CUCKOO. LIKE A SMALL MISSILE OR PROJECTILE, THE COMPOSITOR'S DINGBAT IS THROWN ONTO THE PRINTED PAGE. DIGITI-ZATION HAS MADE IT POSSIBLE TO TRANSFORM DOODLES, PICTOGRAPHS, AND DRAWINGS INTO DINGBAT ALPHABETS. RANGING FROM THE SYMBOLIC TO THE DECORATIVE, GRAPHICAL GADGETS HAVE ADHERED TO CERTAIN TYPE

FAMILIES, WHILE ORPHAN GLYPHS HAVE

TAKEN ON LIVES OF THEIR OWN.

FELLA PARTS, COLLECTIONS OF RANDOM,

AMORPHIC DOODLES, EXEMPLIFY THE DIGITAL

AGE DINGBAT. LIKE COMIC INKBLOTS, THE

SPLOTCHES ARE FLUNG ON THE SCREEN TO

SPRUCE UP (OR WREAK HAVOC ON) A GRAPHIC

DESIGN. FELLA PARTS ARE DISPARATE, MEAN-

INGLESS GLYPHS THAT CAN BE MIXED AND

MATCHED TO MAKE ODD DESIGNS AND ALLUR-

ING PATTERNS. YET MOST PICTORIAL DINGBATS

REPRESENT MORE SPECIFIC IDEAS, AS IN THE

COMPLEMENTARY ICONOGRAPHY IN THE REM-

EDY TYPE FAMILY. THE CARTOON MINIATUR-

IZATIONS AND PARODIES OF UNIVERSAL SIGN

SYMBOLS CAN BE THROWN AROUND THE LET-

TERFORMS FOR PUNCTUATION OR DECORATION.

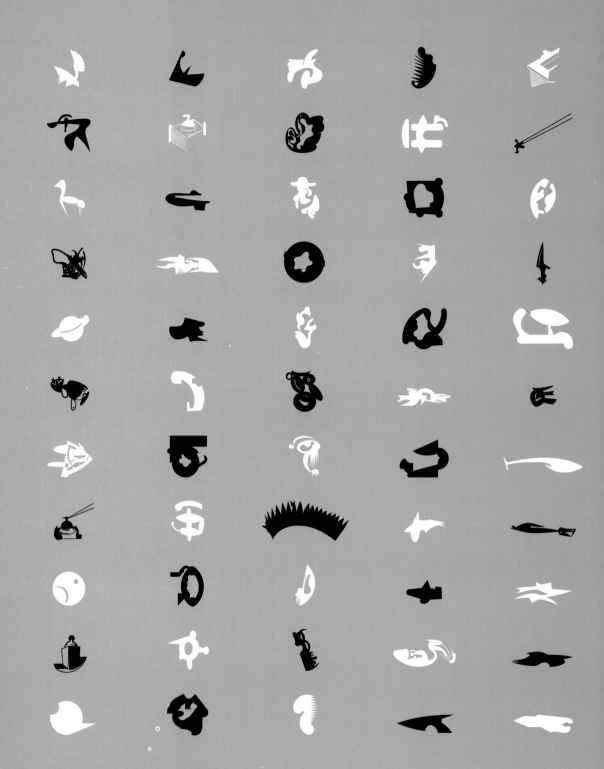

Edward Fella is the guru of the new expressive typography. Fella Parts Regular is the first of a collection of his sketchbook drawings—abstract, anamorphic, and inherently witty designs—that were digitized by Zuzana Licko.

RoarShock One and Two are the first of a projected series of dingbat/border/pattern fonts. Traditionally, fonts have had decorative material designed specifically for them. The title is used to suggest that the apparently abstract characters can be "interpreted."

BOB AUFULDISH

FONTBOY

The fashion for sixties- and seventies-era curlicue hand-drawn lettering began in 1988 with the Thunderjockey's album for the band Living Color and spread. Influenced by this, Remedy is the best drawn, best conceived, and most widely used of the lot.

FRANK HEINE

EMIGRE FONTS

ITC DAVE'S RAVES ONE (1996)

DAVID SAGORSKI

INTERNATIONAL TYPEFACE
CORPORATION

Three hundred "cheeky and charming" spot illustrations drawn from a range of eclectic sources, including vintage clip art, Aztec figures, children's illustrations, and styles and motifs used by Miró, Picasso, and Van Gogh—from sci-fi robots to dancing monkeys.

BIG CHEESE (1992)

ERIC DONELAN &
BOB AUFULDISH

EMIGRE FONTS

This is an experiment in communication processes. The pictograms look like signs yet act as symbols for "nothing in particular." The designers are interested to see what meanings the pictograms acquire over time through use in different contexts.

This collection draws inspiration from printers' stock cuts of the twenties and thirties. As the name suggests, these icons reflect the times—at least the style of contemporary illustration. They can be used to accent a page or tell a complete story.

This is a graphic collection of portraits of "successful dowagers" and the tools of choice by which they assail their unsuspecting spouses. In an epoch when type knows no bounds, the preference in dingbats is for raucousness and hilarity.

ZIETGUYS TWO (1994)

ERIC DONELAN &
BOB AUFULDISH

EMIGRE FONTS

It is not easy to draw images as complex as these to be reproduced at such a small scale. But ZietGuys One and Two are masterpieces of complex simplicity. They are stylistically unified but each glyph tells a different story (or, used together, tells many).

FOUNDRIES ON THE EDGE

The American Type Corp. was founded in 1994 to make locally designed avant-garde type available outside of Indiana. ATC is an alternative to the larger foundries that release hundreds of fonts at rock-bottom prices. "We are a smaller foundry," concedes director Brian Horner, "more concerned with providing type-faces that we feel are informed and up-to-date."

Design: Brian Horner

Design: Brian Horner

Design: Brian Horner

Elliott Peter Earls has published and produced typefaces and printed matter since 1990. His work at Cranbrook Academy of Art led him to form The Apollo Program, a design firm, type foundry, and multimedia studio. His faces are now distributed exclusively through Emigre Fonts. His CD-ROM, "Throwing Apples at the Sun," is the nexus of art and design in an interactive format.

Design: Elliot Earls

Design: Elliot Earls

Design: Elliot Earls

Jeffery Keedy is a pioneer of digital type design. Designed in 1988, Keedy Sans is one of the more venerable specimens in this book. Keedy is on the faculty in the Program in Graphic Design at California Institute of the Arts. His articles have appeared in *EYE*, *I.D.*, *Print*, and *FUSE*. His most recent type designs combine a sense of history and the digital future.

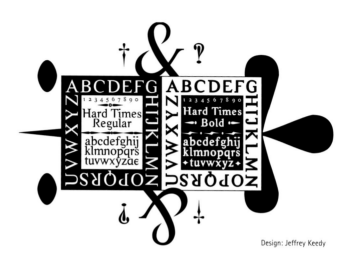

Design: Jeffrey Keedy

Design: Jeffrey Keedy

Design: Jeffrey Keedy

Michael Worthington is the founder of Cookin' Fonts. He describes himself as an English émigré, ex–Cal Arts student. About his typefaces he says, "I guess some people might consider some of these to be a little abnormal." They build, however, on the short legacy of the digital revolution. None of them are entirely finished, but in their various stages of completion they are available as Cookin' Fonts.

Design: Michael Worthington

Design: Michael Worthington

Emigre, Inc. is a digital type foundry and publisher and distributor of graphic design–related software and printed materials. Founded in 1984, coinciding with the birth of the Macintosh, Emigre was one of the first independent type foundries. Emigre holds exclusive license to over 157 original typefaces. For twelve years *Emigre* magazine has been a clarion of the New Typography and a forum for discourse on post modern design.

Design: Rudy VanderLans & Frank Heine

Design: Rudy VanderLans & Mark Andresen

Design: Rudy VanderLans

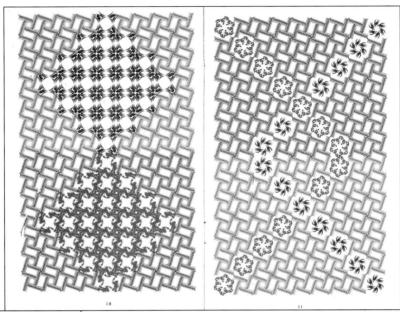

Design: Zuzana Licko

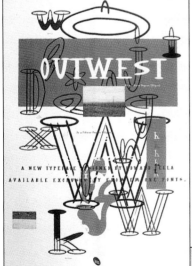

Design: Rudy VanderLans & Edward Fella

Design: Rudy VanderLans

Design: Rudy VanderLans

The Exploding Font Company was founded on July 4, 1996, by book publisher/designer Gary Hustwit as a "vehicle to subversively influence the lives of billions of unsuspecting people." He recruited "graphic terrorists" like Chank "The Traveling Font Salesman" Diesel, Jim "Gomiko" Marcus, Dean "Clean" Vaccaro, and an army of font thugs to help take over the design world. "Exploding fonts have been scientifically formulated to let graphic designers subliminally control their audiences."

Design: Chank Diesel

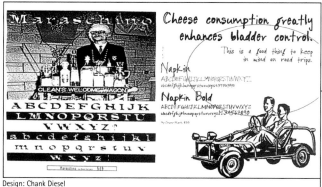

Design: Chank Diesel

uanna be David Carson

109

fontBoy is the creation of Bob Aufuldish, who is a partner in Aufuldish & Warinner. He is also an assistant professor at the California College of Arts and Crafts. fontBoy was launched in 1995 to manufacture and distribute fonts designed by Aufuldish, Kathy Warinner, and others. Their work is an eclectic mix of on-the-edge, over-the-edge, and beyond-the-edge work.

Design: Bob Aufuldish

Design: Bob Aufuldish

Design: Bob Aufuldish

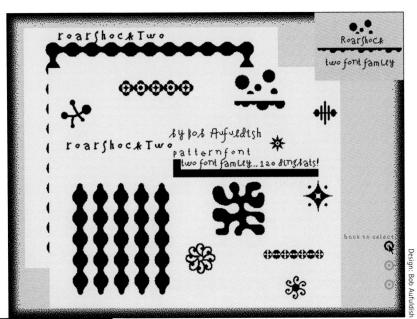

Design: Bob Aufuldish

Design: Bob Aufuldish

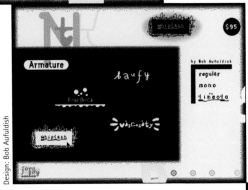

Design: Bob Aufuldish

Design: Bob Aufuldish

The FontShop, founded in Berlin in 1989 by type designer and typographer Erik Spiekermann, began as a network of a variety of type designers. Today the FontShop has offices in many nations. FontBook is a huge resource of digital material referencing over 8,000 fonts (including Eastern European and non-Latin letterforms) and 15,000 symbols and ornaments from more than thirty international font developers. *FUSE* is their multimedia publication of experimental typography, conceived and developed by Neville Brody.

Design: Erik van Blokland & Just van Rossum

Design: John Siddle

Design: John Critchley

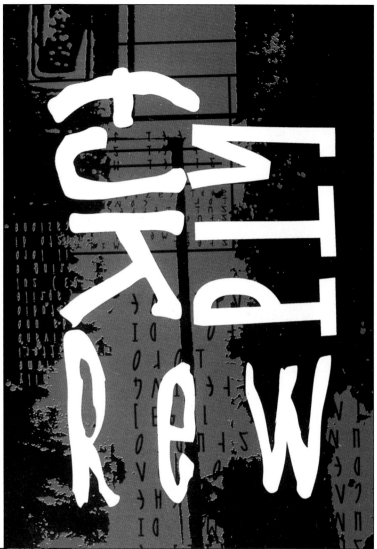

Design: Fabrizio Schiavi

Design: Klaus Dieter Lettau

Design: Neville Brody

An artist raised in a family of writers and printers, Tobias Frere-Jones learned the power of written text, and naturally slipped into the design of letterforms. He graduated Rhode Island School of Design in 1992 and began full-time work for the Font Bureau in Boston, where he is currently a Senior Designer. His most popular types are Interstate and Garage Gothic. He has designed typefaces for numerous newspapers, magazines, and journals (including Hightower for The *AIGA Journal of Graphic Design*).

Design: Tobias Frere Jones

Design: Tobias Frere Jones

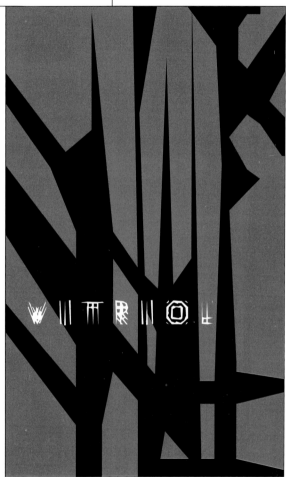

Design: Tobias Frere Jones

Design: Tobias Frere Jones

GARAGE FONTS

Garage Fonts was started in 1993 by David Carson, Betsy Kopshina, and Norbert Schultz. It was intended to be a vehicle for selling unusual and exotic fonts used in *RayGun* magazine. Since its founding, many new designers have helped expand the menu to 100 fonts. With names like Plastered, OakMagicMushroom, Cathodelic, and Ghettout, these faces are definitely not conventional.

Design: Betsy Kopshina

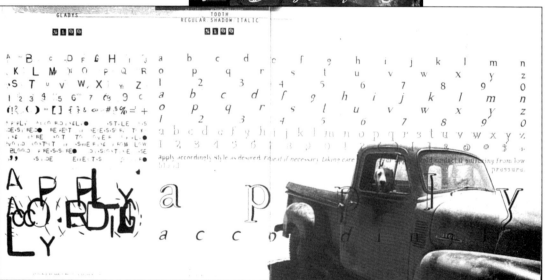

Design: Betsy Kopshina

Design: Betsy Kopshina

Jonathan Hoefler is a typeface designer and an armchair type historian whose New York studio specializes in the design of original typefaces. His work includes faces for *Rolling Stone, Harper's Bazaar, The New York Times Magazine, Sports Illustrated,* and *House and Garden.* He sees his work as "an investigation into the circumstances behind historical form." In each of his designs, he attempts to interpret the critical and aesthetic theories that precipitated a particular style of letter.

Design: Jonathan Hoefler

House Industries began in November of 1993 with the original partners of Brand Design Company in Wilmington, Delaware. The first House Industries type collection was ten original display faces, including Funhouse, Roughouse, and Playhouse. This collection has since grown to over eighty original display faces that take their influence from a wide cultural spectrum. House has begun to focus on developing "theme sets" of fonts, including the Monster Fonts, the Street Van set, the Rat Fink Fonts, the Bad Neighborhood, and the Scrawl collection.

Design: Allen Mercer & Andy Cruz

Design: Allen Mercer & Andy Cruz

Design: Jeremy Dean

LettError was formed in 1989 when Erik van Blokland and Just van Rossum started working together in a small design firm in Berlin. The duo acquired a taste for programming and hacking around with computers before the desktop revolution. "The thing closest to a LettError philosophy is understanding the nature of the tools used in design," they write. The LettError members work separately together in what is sometimes referred to as the "virtual office." There is no real office; much of the work happens at home or on the networks.

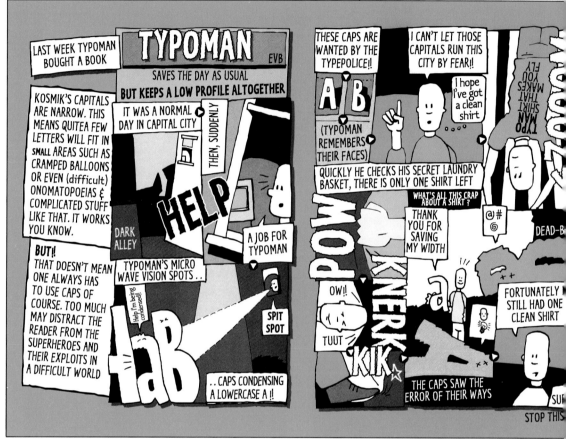

Design: Erik Van Blokland

Design: Erik van Blokland

Plazm Magazine, Portland, Oregon's only internationally distributed art and culture magazine, is the forum for Plazm fonts. Plazm Media was founded in 1991, the "raucous child of a group of artists dissatisfied with available avenues of expression." Like the magazine, which invites work from a wide range of artists with different cultural perspectives, fonts are designed by an equally diverse group of type designers.

Design: Josh Berger

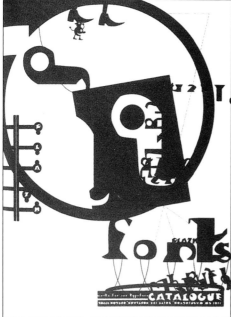

Design: Marcus Burlile

Design: Niko Courtelis

Prototype was founded in late 1994 by Charles Wilkin, owner of Automatic Art and Design in Columbus, Ohio. The earliest offering was a poster featuring eleven fonts. Since then the collection has grown to eighteen fonts, a wide range from scripts to handwritten letters to velvet velour inspired by rave flyers and cyber-punk graphics of Japanese pop culture. All the fonts are designed by Charles Witkin (save two: Blade, designed by Lee Barber, and Glitch, by Keith Tatum, with other designers on the horizon).

Design: Charles Wilkin

Design: Charles Witkin

Design: Charles Witkin

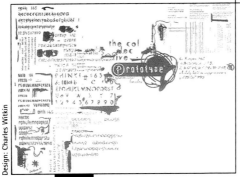

Design: Charles Witkin

Shift was originally concevied by Joshua Distler in 1993 as a way of marketing fonts designed for use in projects by San Francisco Bay Area designers. Since then Shift has offered a small library of fonts with predominantly technological themes. Shift plans to double the size of its current font library. Additions include NucleusOne, Electro, Lumpy, and Slip. Distler's background in computer programming and his fascination with digital media has taken him into realms of New Media.

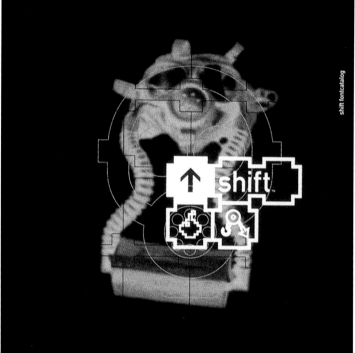

Design: Joshua Distler

Design: Joshua Distler

Design: Joshua Distler

Nancy Mazzei and Brian Kelly, aka Smokebomb, are located in Brooklyn, New York, and have been partners since 1990. They were responsible for the design and art direction of *KGB*, a New York–based alternative culture magazine that showcased both Smokebomb and other digital foundry fonts.

Design: Nancy Mazzei & Brian Kelly

Design: Nancy Mazzei & Brian Kelly

Design: Nancy Mazzei & Brian Kelly

Design: Nancy Mazzei & Brian Kelly

Design: Nancy Mazzei & Brian Kelly

Design: Nancy Mazzei & Brian Kelly

Frustrated by the limits of commercial graphic design, Carlos Segura and Scott Smith decided to form their own type company to reflect changes and improvements in the typographic commuity. Not content with following trends, T-26 has sought to provide an outlet for everything from innovative type ideas to ways of displaying and promoting type. Scott Smith has since left the firm. The company reprsents numerous international graphic and type designers, including students and professionals. Emphasis is placed on experimental and progressive type.

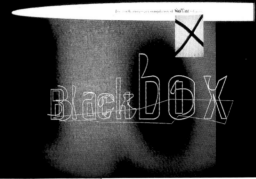

Design: Carlos Segura

Design: Carlos Segura

THE ROCK THE VOTE
KICK-OFF

PARTY
AT THE HARD ROCK CAFE

125

Thirstype is a loosely organized collective of eight typographers. The purpose of the organization is to serve as a voice for artists with ideas "currently unpalatable in established arenas of design and the criticism thereof," writes Chester of Thirstype. Their goal is to cultivate distinct typographic personalities for each artist and to nurture acceptance of a broader definition for visual typographic forms.

Design: Rick Valicenti

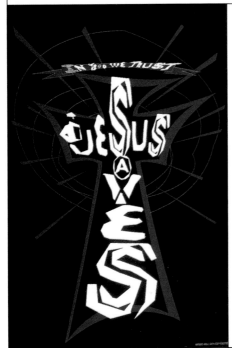

Design: Paul Sych

Design: Rick Valicenti

Design: Rick Valicenti

INDEX

TYPE FACES

THE AMERICAN TYPE CORP.

4749 West 300 North,

Greenfield, Indiana 46140

317 471 5427

317 921 8987 fax

silo4u@inetdirect.net

THE APOLLO PROGRAM

82 East Elm Street,

Greenwich, Connecticut 06830

203 861 7075

203 861 7079 fax

Elliott@the apolloprogram.com

http://www.theapolloprogram.com

COOKIN' FONTS

808 Tularosa Drive #12,

Los Angeles, California 90036

213 953 6123

maxfish@earthlink.net

DE WITT ANTHONY, INC.

126 Main Street,

Northampton, Massachusetts 01060

413 586 4304

413 585 0577

DA@dewittanthony.com

EMIGRE, INC.

4475 D Street,

Sacramento, California 95819

916 451 4344

800 944 9021

916 451 4351 fax

editor@emigre.com

http://www.emigre.com

**THE EXPLODING
FONT COMPANY**

P.O. Box 90100,

San Diego, California 92169

619 234 9429

619 234 9479 fax

explofont@aol.com

http://www.tumyeto.com/exploding

FONTSHOP INTERNATIONAL

Bermanstraße 102,

10961 Berlin, Germany

011 49 30 693 7022

011 49 30 692 8443 fax

info@fontfont.de

http://www.fontfont.de

JEFFERY KEEDY

574 South Ogden Dr.

Los Angeles, California 90036

213 939 6355

Ciphertype@aol.com

U.S. Distributors for FontShop:

FONTSHOP SAN FRANCISCO

350 Pacific Avenue,

San Francisco, California 94111

888 FF-FONTS

415 398-7678

ginger@metadesign.com

MONOTYPE TYPOGRAPHY, INC.

985 Busse Road,

Elk Grove, Illinois 6007-2400

800 MONOTYPE

874 718 0500 fax

sales@monotypeusa.com

http://www.monotype.com

Canadian Distributor for FontShop:

FONTSHOP CANADA

20 Toronto Street #100,

Toronto, Ontario M5C 2B8, Canada

416 364 9164

416 364 1914 fax

fontshopcan@applelink.apple.com

FONTBOY

183 The Alameda,

San Anselmo, California 94960

415 721 7921

415 721 7965 fax

fontboyone@aol.com

aufwar@aol.com

www.well.com/user/bobauf/fontboy.html

TOBIAS FRERE-JONES

175 Newbury Street,

Boston, Massachusetts 02116

617 423 8773

frerejones@fontbureau.co

GARAGE FONTS

P.O. Box 3101,

Del Mar, California 92014

619 755 4561 phone and fax

info@garagefonts.com

http://www.garagefonts.com

THE HOEFLER TYPE FOUNDRY

611 Broadway, Room 815,

New York, New York 10012-2608

212 777 6640

212 777 6684 fax

hoefler@typography.com

http://www.typography.com

HOUSE INDUSTRIES
427 Tatnall Street,
Wilmington, Delaware 19801
800 888 4390
302 888 1650 fax
roat@houseind.com

INTERNATIONAL
TYPEFACE CORPORATION
228 East 45th Street
New York, New York 10017
212 949-8072
212 949-8485 fax
designedit@aol.com
itc@esselte.com
http://www.esselte.com/itc

LETTERROR
Erik van Blokland
Laan van Meerdervoort 1f,
2511 AA Den Haag, Nederland
011 31 70 360 5025
011 31 70 310 6685 fax
evb@knoware.nl
Just van Rossum
Koediefstraat 17,
2511 CK Den Haag, Nederland
011 31 70 362 5147
011 31 70 346 2976 fax
http://www.letterror.com

P. SCOTT MAKELA
3711 Glendale Terrace,
Minneapolis, Minessota 55410
612 922 2271
612 922 2367 fax

PLAZM FONTS
P.O. Box 2863
Portland, Oregon 97208-2863
503 222 6389
503 222 6356 fax
plazmedia@aol.com

PROTOTYPE
2318 North High #9,
Columbus, Ohio 43202
614 447 8013
goproto@aol.com
http://www.prototype-typeo.com

SHIFT
P.O. Box 4,
Burlingame, California 94011-0004
415 737 1004
415 343 3498 fax
fontinfo@shitype.com
http://www.shiftype.com

SMOKEBOMB
106 Norman Avenue,
Brooklyn, New York 11222
718 389 3873
llazzy@.com

STUDIO DAEDALUS
P.O. Box 115212,
Champaign, Illinois 61826-1521
217 398 8443 fax

T-26
1110 North Milwaukee Avenue,
Chicago, Illinois 60622
312 862 1201
312 649 1214 fax
T26font@aol.com
http://www.t26font.co

THIRSTYPE
117 South Cook #333,
Barrington, Illinois 60010
847 842 0222
708 842 0220
thirstype@aol.com

FOUNDRIES